Marketing Strategies for Writers

Michael H. Sedge

ALLWORTH PRESS
NEW YORK

04   03   02   01   00   99   5   4   3   2   1

Published by Allworth Press
An imprint of Allworth Communications
10 East 23rd Street, New York, NY 10010

Cover design by Douglas Design Associates, New York, NY

Page composition/typography by SR Desktop Services, Ridge, NY

ISBN: 1-58115-040-7

Library of Congress Cataloging-in-Publication Data:

Sedge, Michael H.
    Marketing strategies for writers / Michael H. Sedge.
        p. cm.
    Includes bibliographical references and index.
    ISBN 1-58115-040-7 (pbk.)
        1. Authorship--Marketing. I. Title.

    PN161 .S396 1999
    070.5'2--dc21   99-047781

Printed in Canada

CONTENTS

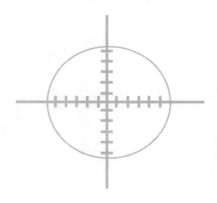

ACKNOWLEDGMENTS

My sincere thanks go out to the following pros: Angela Adair, Gordon Burgett, Andrea Campbell, Alan Caruba, Lisa Collier Cool, Paulette Cooper, Meryl Davids, Ann Douglas, Jack El-Hai, Lynn Grisard Fullman, Wendy Grossman, Katie and Gene Hamilton, Joel Jacobs, Melanie Johnston, John Kremer, Jan Larkey, Charlotte Libov, Leil Lowndes, Downs Matthews, Chris Maturi, Mary Mihaly, Heather Millar, Karen O'Connor, Timothy Perrin, Skip Press, Shirley Sirota Rosenberg, Marilyn and Tom Ross, Elaine Shimberg, and Robyn Spizman.

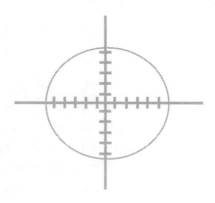

INTRODUCTION

When I first began this project, and throughout its writing, several colleagues questioned why I would spend my time producing yet another work on marketing techniques for authors looking to sell their books. Therefore, I think it is important that I point out "why" here and now.

This book is not, and was never intended to be, a manual for bookselling authors—though much of the advice herein can be applied to that area. There are already several excellent marketing books to aid authors in selling their published titles. Some of these, which I have personally found useful, are listed in the appendix, Resources for the Warrior Writer.

From the outset, this work was intended to provide insight and unique methods for the marketing of writers' work (articles, books, and so on), services, and self. This is an area in which many writers fall short; it is a niche that required filling, and I believe this book fills it well.

As part of my research, I conducted an informal survey of professional nonfiction writers. What I discovered is that freelancers enjoying an annual income of $40,000 or more traditionally spend at least 40 percent of their time marketing their writing to today's top-paying editors. Those making $60,000 and above tend to supplement their income by jobs other than writing—for example, teaching or public speaking. It is my hope that after reading this book and applying the techniques outlined here, you too will be among the ranks of writers making a comfortable living from their talents.

I've explained my way of doing business in these pages. There were times when I questioned if I should reveal certain tactics—for instance, calling editors pretending to be Mr. Sedge's secretary and wanting to book an appointment with the editor-in-chief. In the end, I am pleased that I did, for this is true warrior marketing! Not the fancy query, the college textbook-style, or the traditional method of selling your words. Today's markets, in reality, require more. They call for you to be ruthless, sly, and to take no prisoners.

Some veteran writers may disagree with, if not disapprove of, some of the techniques and suggestions I make. Some already have. In most cases, however, these writers are enjoying leisurely lives as contributing editors to top-paying publications and the monthly paychecks that come with that turf. For the other 99 percent—those freelancers who struggle to make a living—it's a war out there. And as the old saying goes, all's fair in love and war . . . and writing.

—Michael Sedge
Naples, Italy

P.S. During your reading, take notes. It will be much easier to come back to the advice, tips, and examples you wish to apply to your particular situation if you underline them with a highlighter pen. Then, mark the page with a Post-it. By the time you finish the book, you'll have a complete marketing plan at your fingertips.

Oh, one more thing: If the Post-its are camouflaged, that's even better.

LET THE WAR BEGIN

In the summer heat of a University of La Verne classroom, I looked out into the attentive faces of fifty-two students—each one eager to learn the secrets of becoming a successful freelance writer. Being a writer, for some, was a passing flirt. For others, it was a lifelong dream.

"I cannot teach you to write," I began, pausing just long enough to enjoy their reactions. "But assuming you have the basic skills required to be a writer, I *can* teach you to sell yourself and your work."

From the back of the room, a young lady timidly raised her hand.

"Yes?"

"Mr. Sedge, what do you mean, 'sell yourself'? I'm starting to feel like a prostitute."

Following a round of laughter, I explained that, thirty or forty years ago, a writer's talent alone was enough to launch a career. Unfortunately, the days of Faulkner, Fitzgerald, and Hemingway are far behind us. In today's overwhelmingly competitive markets, one's ability to put words on paper is, in itself, no longer sufficient. Contemporary editors have neither the time nor the desire to nurture writers; most are too busy trying to climb the corporate ladder in hopes of acquiring their own imprint or executive position. They send new scribes to agents who, in turn, seek talented individuals with "track records."

It's the "Circle of Success" syndrome. You need an agent to get your material read by editors, but you can't get an agent unless you have a track record. You can't get a track record unless editors read and publish your material. And all the time you know your work is as good as, or better than, 50 percent of the titles occupying the shelves of Barnes & Noble.

On the periodical front, the scene is not much better. Each day, editors receive hundreds of thousands of queries and manuscripts, allowing them to be so selective—and pay, in many cases, rates that make minimum wage look attractive—that writers, from time to time, begin to feel as if they are running into brick walls. In addition, most editors have a stable of writers from whom they buy most of their features and to whom they pass most of their assignments.

Sure, there are exceptions. Take, for example, Stephen King. His first book, *Carrie*, became a bestseller almost overnight. I once interviewed King and asked him what it was about *Carrie* that made it so phenomenally successful. His answer: "Right place, right time, right product." He then explained that his prosperity came thanks to the film *The Exorcist*. The American public was hungry for supernatural horror after the box-office success of this movie, and King had a mind full of terror to offer.

The chances that such luck of the draw will happen to you is about the same as you picking the $25 million lotto numbers next week. And yet, a large percentage of would-be successful writers merely sit back and wait for a magical moment like this to occur. Personally, where success is involved, I don't believe in magic, in winning lottery tickets, or even in luck of the draw. I believe that in today's market-place you create your own success, you make your paths, and you fight the odds with marketing techniques that make editors and publishers want your work.

Yes, that's right. You make *them* want *you*.

We Want You!

The ultimate example of this can be seen in Monica Lewinsky. Prior to the affair with President Clinton, U.S. media were more interested in Homer Simpson than this White House intern. When news of the relationship broke, she became an overnight celebrity. Requests poured in from producers of television and radio talk shows around the country. Periodicals, so it seemed, could not get enough of her—unfortunately, Kenneth Starr had exclusive rights at the time. Following the independent counsel's investigation, an army of publishers came waving seven-figure advances for the book rights to her story. (Personally, I still prefer Homer.)

I am not suggesting that you spend time with the president in the room adjacent to the Oval Office. My point here is that editors, publishers, and other media people are human beings. The psychology of marketing will work on them, just as it works on millions of people every day. When we watch television and hear about McDonald's, Coca-Cola, and Intel day after day after day after day, our minds automatically resonate with these products. When we drive down the street and get an urge for something to eat, Golden Arches begin to flash in our minds. It's not a conscious decision derived from logical thought but, rather, psychological marketing, like a drug, beginning to take its effect.

For years, AT&T has taken advantage of psychological marketing, to the point where a large percentage of Americans are unwilling to give up their telephone service with this company, despite competition offering identical quality and lower prices. During the late 1980s and early 1990s, I was the European director for MCI Communications' military marketing. My primary job was selling MCI's WorldPhone Card to service members and their families. MCI's rates were consistently 3¢ to 6¢ cents a minute lower than AT&T's, depending on what country one was calling from. MCI's ads highlighted this point to potential customers.

How did AT&T counter this? Simply by running ads that stated, "But they are not AT&T—the company you've grown up with."

That one line told the story. People *wanted* AT&T, they related to AT&T, they were comfortable with AT&T.

Similarly, part of your business as a writer is to make potential clients feel so confident in your ability that they select you over the competition. Accomplishing this is not difficult. It does, however, require skillful marketing. I recently surveyed fifty full-time, freelance writers and discovered that individuals dedicating 40 percent or more of their time to aggressive marketing enjoyed far more success and financial rewards than their "I'm a writer, so I just write" counterparts.

"Marketing is the key to the career. If I don't market, I don't write."

—*Timothy Perrin, author of five books and over 150 articles*

What category do you fit into? Are you content observing the war on CNN from the comfort of your living room, or would you prefer to be on the battlefield? If you choose the latter, then pull out your camouflage fatigues, arm yourself with a semiautomatic computer, and prepare for battle. Your goal is simple: Increase your income by increasing the quality and quantity of your clientele. To achieve this, you will cover three battlefields: (1) promoting your work, (2) promoting your business, and (3) promoting yourself.

> "I have increased my income by 30 percent this year by getting better at marketing."
> —*Heather Millar, professional writer*

You are about to become a warrior. Use guerrilla warfare, take no prisoners, and employ every tactic in the combat manual—and some that are not. Today's media business is a jungle, and there's a war going on in it. If you intend to win the battle, you *must* become a marketing warrior.

In many ways, contemporary marketing techniques are like military maneuvers. Each time you set out to conquer a new client, obtain an assignment, or sell a proposal or a completed work, you are going into battle. Little did I realize, during my four years of active military duty, three years as a military reporter for The Associated Press, and eight years as a foreign correspondent for *Armed Forces Journal International,* that I was merely laying the groundwork for future marketing activities. Military strategies, battle plans, intelligence reports, offensive lines, and assaults all parallel the marketing world.

The Warrior at Work

In March 1999, the Discovery Channel aired a special on Cleopatra highlighting the recently explored sunken city of this last Egyptian queen. Simultaneously, the Discovery Channel Books, in cooperation with Random House, released a title on this subject. I was part of the team selected to work on this project. It was not by chance that I received the assignment but, rather, it was the result of a long-term, thought-out battle plan.

It had taken me more than a year and a variety of marketing techniques to break into the Discovery Channel. I used networking—much like a military strategist uses spies—to obtain inside information about new developments in the company. This is how I learned about the Discovery Channel's upcoming book division and other areas where writers might be required. Knowing such information allowed me to fill the company's immediate needs before word got out and competition became overwhelming. I was able to obtain lists of future programming from the advertising department (intelligence reports). My "insiders" also provided me with names, telephone numbers, and e-mail addresses. From this "inside information" I noted that the newly appointed director of books was Rita Mullin.

In the early 1980s, I had done work for Time-Life Books. At that time there was a Rita Mullin working for the company. Suddenly—*bingo*—I had an introduction! Even if she turned out to be a different Rita Mullin, it was a perfectly good way to initiate a dialogue. But what was my goal? Other than asking if she was the ex-Time-Life editor, what did I hope to achieve? I had to have a plan, as if I were going into battle.

Editors are busy people and there is nothing more distracting than a writer dropping by "just to say hello." They need ideas, offers, something concrete that will generate enthusiasm and interest long after you've left their office. Having a well-defined marketing (battle) plan will, therefore, serve you as well as the editor.

In my case the goal was simple: Obtain a book contract from the Discovery Channel. But what should the subject matter be? I was already armed with the long-term TV program scheduling and, from insider reports, knew that the book division would be following this in order to market book/video packages. As I reviewed the network's future program plans, one of the topics that seemed to leap from the pages was Cleopatra. I'd recently read of a French explorer who had found the ancient city of the Ptolemaïs—where Cleopatra and Marc Antony lived out their legendary love affair—submerged in the eastern harbor of Alexandria, Egypt.

I allowed my subconscious to work with this for a couple of days and, finally, came up with a simple marketing strategy:

1. E-mail Rita Mullin a "remember me" letter and update her on my professional activities (break the ice)
2. Immediately find a market for an article on the Cleopatra research in Egypt
3. Continue correspondence with Mullin
4. Send a press kit on my activities to Mullin
5. Get known around the Discovery Channel
6. After publication of the Cleopatra article, visit the Discovery Channel in Bethesda (meeting with Rita)

The following day, two queries went out. The first was to Rita, the second to Jim Randall, editor of *Compass,* Mobil Oil's in-house publication. Jim had purchased several articles from me over the past decade, many dealing with ocean activities. This one seemed right for them and, ultimately, he commissioned the Cleopatra story.

Steps one and two accomplished.

Rita, it turned out, *was* the ex-Time-Life editor, making our continued correspondence easier—after all, we shared a common background and, therefore, had mutual respect for one another.

Step three accomplished.

I intentionally avoided sending useless messages to her, trying to spread them out so as not to become annoying. We discussed her new position; her hopes as book editor, and, very vaguely, the editorial direction of the Discovery Channel Books. At one point, I nonchalantly asked, "Would you mind if I sent you samples of my work, in the event you ever need a writer?" She agreed, setting the stage for step four.

Just as battlefield commanders plan out the armor, the aircraft, and the troops that will go into an assault, I spent hours contemplating what would go into the "press kit." Rita was expecting a few clips. What she received was a professionally printed, four-color folder with a matching business card and stationery inside; a brief, one-and-a-half–page biography highlighting my best work; and, printed on heavy, cream-toned bond paper, two four-color feature articles—one on underwater archaeology in Italy, another on iceberg research—and a copy of my book, *Commercialization of the Oceans.* To be even more impressive, I sent it UPS rather than standard mail.

Nearly seven months had now gone by and my insiders continued to feed me information. To accomplish step five, I had corresponded with the Discovery Channel Online editors (the company's Internet site) about article ideas. I had also wedged my way into the PR department by selling three stories on the Discovery Channel-related topics—including a profile of the founder and CEO and two pieces on the company's new travel adventures. I had contacted several company executives as well as foreign offices for quotes. At this point, my name had become familiar to many of the Discovery Channel decision makers.

In the fall of 1998, my article *In Search of Cleopatra* made the cover of the *Compass.* It was now time for the assault. I sent a message to Rita informing her that I planned to be in the area and would like to meet her. Ten days later, with troops lined up and guns loaded, I sat in the Bethesda office of the Discovery Channel sipping coffee and lowered my guns to fire the first shot: "How closely will book projects follow the TV programming?"

"Very closely," she replied.

"The reason I ask," I said, reaching into my briefcase, "is because I noticed a program on Cleopatra scheduled for next year. I spent several months writing a story for Mobil Oil on the underwater discovery of Cleopatra's palace by French archaeologist Franck Goddio."

At that point, I handed her a copy of the magazine, which contained the impressive, full-color, seven-page cover story.

"You've worked with Goddio? This is fabulous. We are planning a book on Cleopatra and a large part of it will cover his work—the archaeological finds!"

I simply smiled, as my smoking gun cooled. The first round was obviously mine.

Two weeks later Rita informed me that she would "like to move to the next stage." That is, from mere discussions to putting something on paper. Ultimately, my year-long efforts resulted in a $14,000 contract and an all-expenses-paid, two-week research trip to Egypt.

Good planning. Good execution. Good results. It's all part of the marketing war writers must engage in to be successful. You must be one step ahead of the competition and two steps ahead of your client. So grab your gear and let's hit the road, the war is about to begin.

THE BASICS OF MARKETING

When I was young, growing up in Michigan, I spent many winters constructing giant snowballs. There was something exciting about taking a tiny ball of icy, well-packed snow and rolling it into a boulder too large to budge. A writing career, in some respects, is very similar to creating snowballs. It begins small. As you work and your clientele grows, so does the size of your snowball. The more visibility you achieve, the more work you are offered and the faster the sphere rolls. While most writers continue on a slow, steadily growing path, there are those—albeit very few—who, often quite surprisingly, come to a high peak, looking down into a snow-covered valley. For them, a single push sends their tiny snowball effortlessly down the mountainside, picking up momentum, growing as it goes, until it is too heavy to be moved by a single individual.

Blessed are those whose snowball reaches this stage, for they are in the elite company of such names as Clancy, Cornwell, Grisham, King, and Steel. At this point in their careers, there is no need for them to market their work; others will do it for them. Marketing opportunities will fall upon them like snowflakes. Some offers they will accept, resulting in even more self-rolling snowballs. Other opportunities they will decline, causing the snow to melt.

"Marketing is much more important today than it was when I began my writing career more than 30 years ago."

—*Elaine Shimberg, author of* Write Where You Live

In addition to my writing career, I spent nearly six years as the director of MCI Communications' military marketing for Europe and the Middle East. One of the responsibilities of that position was to coordinate sponsored celebrity tours at U.S. military installations abroad. During an interview with Tom Clancy for an article in Singapore Airlines' *Silver Kris* magazine, I asked if he'd be interested in such a tour.

"I don't have the time to even consider it. My plate is just too full."

Obviously, Clancy's snowball was so large that he alone could not budge it.

For most of us "earthbound" writers, however, there is always room for growth—in the form of increased exposure, additional work, career advancement, and greater pay. Your professional snowball may just be starting—small enough to hold in your hand. Or you may already have years of experience and a sphere larger than a basketball. No matter what your individual situation, whether you are a novice or a veteran writer, coming up with and executing effective marketing strategies will launch your career into new heights of exposure and employment.

Just how fast your snowball grows is up to you. Whether it moves at the pace of freezing water or races forward like a sled on an icy track depends on you. It is you, and you alone, who will determine whether your career remains a snowball or becomes an avalanche. No one has more interest in your success than you do. So if you do not take a proactive role in promoting your work and yourself, no one else will either.

A writing career without marketing skills is similar to making snowballs with freshly fallen snow—it simply does not work. There is no substance, no "packing" power. Just as you create a tiny ball, it falls apart, and you find yourself starting all over again.

Understanding the psychology of marketing should therefore be as important to you as your writing ability; these two factors will determine the future of your professional career. Everything you do to sell your work—from addressing an envelope and printing a manuscript, to teaching a local seminar and having lunch with an editor—is marketing.

---

mar•ket•ing *n.* 1. All business activity required in buying or selling a product or service, including communicating, advertising, packaging, shipping, pricing, etc.

Last week, for instance, and despite protest from my wife, I purchased a new computer. I explained to her that the new machine would allow me to better format, edit, and print my work with varied fonts, thus enhancing the appearance of manuscripts. Receiving such professional-looking packages, editors would subconsciously have a positive impression of my work even before they read it. This, in turn, would increase my chances of a sale.

In short, the new computer was part of my marketing strategy. In addition, I said, the cost could be deducted from our taxes. Whether she believed me or not, I now have a new Compaq.

College professors will tell you that there are six parts to marketing:

1. Identifying a need
2. Service/product strategy—that is, setting yourself apart from the crowd
3. Informing potential buyers of the product and/or services
4. Packaging and distribution
5. Price determination
6. Customer service

Inasmuch as each of these areas will be discussed at greater length in subsequent chapters, it is sufficient at this point for you to understand the existence of each aspect of marketing. Lacking knowledge in one or more of these categories can greatly damage your chances for both short- and long-term sales. Early in my career, for instance, I was given an assignment by the Japanese magazine *Mini World*. Upon completion of the article, I packaged it, with photographs, and sent it airmail to the editor. Two weeks later, and a day after deadline, the package had still not arrived. As a result, the editor was placed in a difficult position, my professionalism was questioned, and my services were never called upon again. Why? I had not given serious consideration to the "distribution" aspect of marketing.

In an effort to save money, I had opted for the postal service over a more costly, but faster and more secure, courier delivery. Because the work was going to an overseas client, I would have made the deadline, the sale, and, in the long run, probably received future assignments had I utilized Federal Express or UPS delivery. I had broken one of the six rules of marketing and, as a result, my relationship and future with this publication suffered.

The Psychology of Marketing

Marketing, as we know it today, feeds on our subconscious desires to be associated with high-quality products and the people who create them. Understanding and properly following the six steps of successful marketing will go a long way toward generating this positive rapport between you and your clients. Editors will want to work with you—buying your articles and books as well as offering assignments when they need a writer—if you properly market and produce yourself and your work. However, not taking the right steps—or doing the job halfway—will have just the opposite effect, as illustrated above.

Rohn Engh, photo marketing wizard and author of *Sell and Re-Sell Your Photos,* says, "Knowledge is useless unless it is applied. That's the first thing novices learn when they venture into the business world. Photographers [and writers] who succeed do so not because of their knowledge of photography [or writing], or photo [and article] marketing, but because they apply what they know."

The level of your success is frequently proportional to your dedication to marketing. I personally feel that you should divide your time evenly between writing and marketing—that is, a fifty-fifty balance. One cannot survive without the other. For a writer to be prosperous, both marketing and writing skill are equally important.

I also believe that all writers should have some marketing background. Adult education classes are an excellent source for obtaining such knowledge—in addition to this book, of course. One of the nice aspects of structured courses is that you can immediately apply what you have learned and, within weeks, have positive or negative feedback to share with instructors and fellow students.

One thing that very few, if any, marketing classes teach, however, is that it is all right to fail. This is only natural, since you are paying for knowledge that should lead to success. And yet, failure is part of every marketing campaign. You should not be discouraged by or afraid of failure. Each time your marketing efforts flop, you are building toward future success. You are learning what does and does not work in your specific field. All good business executives hope for total success, but rejoice when 60 percent of their efforts pay off. Perhaps Joseph Heller, in his book *Catch-22*, best illustrated this when he wrote, "Before the war he was an alert, hard-hitting aggressive marketing executive. As such, he was a very bad marketing executive. Colonel Cargill was so awful a marketing executive that his services were much sought after by firms eager to establish losses for tax purposes."

There obviously is a market for everyone and everything.

As a writer, your marketing methods will be unique. We shall focus on various "tricks" of the trade as we move through the pages ahead. Knowing the psychology and techniques behind traditional marketing will allow you to target your own sales efforts, broaden your market base, and boost your professional career to a plateau where opportunities will ultimately come to you. This should be your goal. Once you have achieved this level of success, you will find yourself at the zenith of the literary mountain looking down into the beautiful, snow-covered valley. You then merely need to push your snowball and watch as it effortlessly rolls downward, growing as it goes.

The Business Image

In 1978 my first article appeared in *Off Duty Europe*, a give-away magazine distributed to U.S. military installations overseas. Upon seeing my name in print, there was the immediate "high" that most writers experience at such moments. I still experience this emotion each time I see my byline on a new feature or book.

Like many freelance writers, I took that initial sale—and all of $82.50—as a sign of success, and proceeded to submit new query letters to editors across the country. Eighty-two rejections later, I decided that something was definitely wrong in my approach and that my *Off Duty* sale had merely been a fluke. While wrong about the latter, I was correct in the assessment of the way I was doing business.

Fortunately, for me, I encountered Charles Leocha at this point in my career. Charlie was publishing a digest-sized magazine at that time, called *New Entertainer,* for the U.S. and NATO military communities in Naples, Italy. I learned many things from Leocha—who has since gone on to become a successful book publisher—and eventually worked for him as an associate editor. Without a doubt, the greatest of these lessons was that you must operate like a business if you hope to be successful. It is not enough, in today's competitive marketplace, to simply be a "freelance writer." You must also be the chief executive officer, the sales and marketing manager, the accountant, and the secretary. But most important, you must think like a business rather than an individual.

I specifically recall one morning in the office of *New Entertainer;* a would-be publisher by the name of Ramon Hernandez asked Leocha how many people it took to start a magazine. His reply: "One, as long as the individual is business-minded."

Years before, Charles Leocha had established himself as World Leisure Corporation. His letterhead, his business cards, his invoices, and his product projected the World Leisure Corporation name and logo. Therefore, while conducting day-to-day business with Leocha, clients felt they were dealing with the large, international, World Leisure Corporation conglomerate. All of this, based on a name and business structure.

All individuals, including editors, want to do business with stable, professional people. Working under the umbrella of a company provides potential clients with a sense of security, false as it may be. It is this psychological illusion that you, as a writer, must appeal to if you are to be successful.

Following Leocha's advice, and tips from a few adult-education business courses, I transformed my freelance operation into an editorial service business under the name of Strawberry Media, Inc. (Yes, there is a reason for the name. I live in the city of Afragola, which, in Italian, means "the land of strawberries." Believe it or not, some editors have picked up on this. And those who do not, always seem to remember the "strawberry man.")

Because I am also a photographer, my letterhead, business cards, and presentation folders—in which all articles and photos are delivered—become instant marketing tools, carrying the logos for Strawberry Media Editorial and Strawberry Media Photos. In recent years, my business has expanded to also include Strawberry Media Promotions and Strawberry Media Communications. While my mainstay is always writing, simply listing these alternative services has greatly increased my annual income through photography, advertising, and marketing work.

The long-term goal of any good business plan is to consistently expand your market share. As such, don't hesitate to increase your services whenever possible, whether you offer copy writing, corporate reports, or even speeches. Your clientele should grow according to the increased services you offer and the projected size and appearance of your business. I began working for regional magazines, for example, and ultimately landed such clients as AT&T, Bank-America, H&R Block, Holiday Inn, and MCI Communications.

Because I live in Europe, I also list two business addresses—my own and that of my parents in Tennessee. Suddenly, in the eyes of potential clients, I operate not only a multiservice company, but also an impressive international agency. That is exactly the impression I want them to have.

One of the primary reasons to operate under a business title rather than your own name is image. When you reach a certain level of professionalism, image plays a major role in your success, or lack of it. I received my first assignments from the Discovery Channel and *Newsweek,* which were both looking to contract a professional editorial business rather than an individual freelancer. One editor confided in me: "Our executives and accounting people feel more comfortable dealing with businesses."

For most writers, operating as a sole proprietor is the easiest business structure. Because your marketing goal is to appear as large as possible, however, you may want to look into other company structures. A perfect example of a writer-turned-business is Arizona-based Melanie Johnston.

"Ten years ago," she explains, "I founded Johnston Writing & Design, a sole proprietorship that provides corporate writing and design services to companies large and small. Corporations seem more comfortable dealing with an entity rather than 'this writer I know.' I believe I'm treated with greater respect than if I were simply a 'freelancer,' which, unfortunately, to many means you write for a hobby."

When selecting a business title, you may want to consider a name other than your own—though many of today's top-rated corporations began as family names. Look into names that would have global impact, something that would fit the twenty-first century. Review some of the multinational company names being used today—CNN International, MSNBC, United Press International, WorldCom—for inspiration and ideas. I also suggest a flashy, eye-catching company logo.

More information on how you can set up a sole proprietorship in your state, including the DBA (doing business as) rules, can be obtained by calling or visiting your local chamber of commerce and/or better business bureau.

Many writers, including myself, have optioned to work as a corporation. To most people, for example, Jack Ryan Enterprises, Ltd., means very little other than the fact that it is a corporation. If I told you that this company owns the copyright to such works as *The Hunt For Red October, Clear and Present Danger,* and *Red Storm Rising,* you would probably realize that Jack Ryan Enterprises, Ltd., is, by another name, Tom Clancy. In a 1996 interview, Clancy explained to me that his pre–best-seller life as a financial consultant provided him with a better understanding of business than that possessed by most writers.

Another author, Andrew Rosenbaum, a specialist in European business and Web site consulting, works under the corporate title Allegra Communications. "It offers considerable fiscal and business advantages," he says. "One has much more flexibility in handling social security and taxes. And publishers process invoices from companies differently than those of sole proprietors. And since I do a lot of international work, it simplifies payment."

Personally, I have owned and operated three companies during the past twenty years. While paperwork increases when you incorporate, there are certain liability protections with this type of business—particularly as you expand and become more successful. It is extremely simple to set up a corporation, including state and federal registration. In fact, it can be done by phone or Internet. Two organizations offering this service—both of which I have used and highly recommend—are Delaware Registry, Ltd. (Tel: (800) 321-2677), and The Company, Corp. (Tel: (800) 542-2677). Internet users can request information through the appropriate Web sites at *www.delreg.com* and *www.ftsbn.com/~incorporate/the company_corporation.htm*. You can also request information by e-mail at *corp@delreg.com* and *companycorp@ftsbn.com*.

If you decide to incorporate, be sure you fully understand the five types of business structures under this system and select the right one for you. The advisers of Delaware Registry, Ltd., and The Company Corp. can explain each of these.

Another alternative, which fits the needs of many writers, is the Limited Liability Company (LLC). As one business-owner-writer put it: "I like that there are no corporate taxes to calculate and pay. And the big plus is that our private assets are protected and separate from the LLC."

A business front is often the only thing separating a "freelance" writer from today's top corporate clients. Establishing yourself as a business should therefore be a priority in your marketing strategy. Once this is accomplished you can better focus on the challenge of conquering new clients and coming up with creative techniques to win over editors. The key factor, for now, is that you begin to think of yourself as a business. For that is what you are, or should be. With this mentality and the advice that follows, your success will widen like a river that has reached the open sea. Dan Poynter, owner of Para Publishing, put it very simply when he said, "Having a business, is just good business."

Internet users can find general small business information, including answers to common questions and 675 searchable pages, at *www.bizproweb.com*. Other sites that offer helpful tips and guidelines for home businesses include *www.bizoffice.com* and *www.smartbiz.com*.

Exploring the Waters

Marketing can often be intimidating and even frightening. To the inexperienced, it's like swimming in unknown waters. In reality, with a well-designed marketing plan and focused target goals, you can slowly explore the waters—slipping in one foot first, then an entire leg, followed by total immersion.

In 1993, while sitting in on a meeting at MCI Communications, I listened as a marketing executive outlined a $1.2 million idea to bring a free concert to U.S. service members in Europe. After the presentation, I suggested testing the concept with a small, target audience; for example, a single base in Germany. If the returns—that is, MCI WorldPhone Calling Card applications—were good, they could then move forward with the larger production. I suddenly found myself up against the power players of the company and withdrew quietly.

Six months later, MCI's *Cool, Country, Comedy and Cowboys* road tour—consisting of over one hundred people, including Miss U.S.A. Kenya Moore, singer Mary J. Blige, country vocal group Pirates of the Mississippi, *Saturday Night Live* comedian James Stephens III, and three members of the Dallas Cowboys football team—hit the streets of Europe. Of the twelve shows, three were ultimately cancelled for lack of sufficient ticket sales. Of the anticipated 40,000 new MCI customers the Washington executive had projected from his "ivory tower," only 1 percent materialized. Now that, my friend, is frightening!

My goal in the pages ahead is to give you an overview of market planning as well as techniques and methods to best implement your plan. We'll then focus on narrowing your scheme into smaller "action plans," just as a battle commander sections off his targets and sends in teams to each area. This will allow you to test-market your strategy before spending a great deal of time and money on methods that are not successful for you.

Publishing Is Marketing

Whether you realize it or not, if you are a published writer, you are already working along one of the most lucrative roads to self-promotion and marketing. Quite simply, publishing *is* marketing. Any time you get your name in print and your work read by mass audiences, you are becoming much better known in your field. Most writers, however, fail to capitalize on their published works.

Recently, for example, I was interviewed for *Writer On Line,* an Internet magazine for writers. The focus of the story was my experience in international sales and my new book *The Writer's and Photographer's Guide to Global Markets.* A few months later, my friend and colleague, British author Jeremy Josephs, was also interviewed. This morning Jeremy wrote saying that while he agreed to the interview, he was not getting much out of it financially. Obviously, I thought, he was not looking at this golden opportunity through a marketer's eyes. I sent the following reply:

> While you are correct in that the token $50 offered by the publisher hardly seems worth the effort, I was able to turn my story into a moneymaker. I first used the Internet address of the story as a "signature" at the bottom of my e-mails, so editors I communicate with could read about me. Second, I cut a deal with the

Writer On Line publisher to print a monthly "Going Global with Mike Sedge" column (about 500 words). Using my name in the title will promote "me" each month. The column will also promote my book. Additionally, *Writer On Line* will have an order form linked to the column, whereby readers can order the book. The publisher also agreed to host a personal Web page for me, at no cost, and to run a banner on the front page of *Writer On Line,* which will also link to the book order form. Finally, I got him to agree to $75 a column.

Paying for the above services—that is, a personal Web page, a book order page, a banner, and so on—would have cost approximately $4,800 a year. Using the initial article as an introduction, I was able not only to avoid these costs, but to reap about $2,400 a year from book sales and the column fees—bringing my total annual savings to $7,200. Then there is the added value of constant Internet exposure, which is hard to put a price on.

Later we'll explore more ways to use your published works as marketing tools, including getting on today's popular television talk shows simply by authoring topical magazine articles. For now, however, you should concentrate on "thinking" like a marketer. Opportunities are everywhere. The difference between success and failure is often your ability to recognize and take advantage of these situations.

CUSTOMER NEEDS

For me, it all started in Ms. Parrett's fourth-hour English class. I was then a handsome, seventeen-year-old captain of the Kearsley High School wrestling team and, in all honesty, an average student. That is, with the exception of English, where I always seemed to excel.

Even then, I had a keen ability to focus on what others needed and, when it was to my advantage, I took the appropriate steps to fulfill these requirements—two basic concepts of marketing. In the case of Ms. Parrett—who had moved to Michigan from California after a heated divorce—needs ran from someone to carry heavy bags to a sympathetic ear to listen to her "I-was-in-Los-Angeles-during-the-hippie-movement-and-understand-what-today's-kids-think" stories.

While my friends called me a "brownnose," when grades were dished out, my plate always seemed to contain a little more than the other average students. What I did not realize then was that I was building the foundation of what would eventually become a profitable marketing career. And, yes, I also learned enough about writing in that and subsequent classes to allow me to publish more than 2,600 articles and several books to date.

At that early age I was already applying the laws of marketing. Ms. Parrett had a need (help with carrying bags, someone to listen). I was fulfilling this need (carrying the bags, listening). In exchange I was "paid" with an extra + if not an entire grade jump. Because of this, I was labeled a "brownnose" by my fellow students. Eighteen years later, *Entrepreneur* magazine would redefine my behavior, calling me a "marketing wizard."

Identify a Need

The first thing you must do to achieve marketing success is to step into the shoes of your customer, figuratively speaking. Daniel Goleman, author of the best-selling book, *Working with Emotional Intelligence,* suggests that individuals with high emotional intellect have a knack for listening to and understanding the points of view of others. They also possess the ability, says Goleman, to utilize the knowledge and insight they gain from listening and to get ahead or achieve, whereas many others might fail. You want to be among those individuals who succeed. By listening and understanding the needs of your clients, you will.

Whether you are trying to get on national television or a radio talk show or to sell an article, a nonfiction book, or a novel, you must always take the approach of "How can I help you?" rather than "How can you help me?" Magazine editors have a number of pages to fill each month. Book editors must generate a certain number of projects each year. Producers require a steady flow of guests to fill their television and radio lineups. You, on the other hand, are there to fulfill these needs with your writing skill and/or availability to appear. This can also be carried over into numerous other areas. If you enjoy speaking, for example, you may find that local schools are looking for an experienced writer/teacher, or perhaps a group needs someone to lecture. Opportunities for promoting your work and yourself are nearly endless.

> "Marketing is an essential enterprise for any professional writer. If you do not introduce other important people to your abilities, strengths, and published work, how will they know you can deliver what you promise? With each subsequent product—I refer to all my work as products—I try to become familiar with what that particular publisher needs in the future."
>
> —*Andrea Campbell, author of* Helping Hands: Monkey Helpers for the Disabled

For me, the "fill a need" concept is so important that I recently added the following catch phrase to my company stationery: "Our job is to make your job easier." This phrase came about after an editor who had commissioned a $5,000 job called to explain that due to editorial changes, a total rewrite would be required. She went on to say, in an apologetic tone, that according to the contract I was required to do this at no extra cost.

"Mary," I replied, "my job is to make your job easier. If a rewrite is needed, a rewrite you will get."

She was thrilled. Not only had I filled her existing need, but I had removed the "bad guy" burden from her shoulders. In doing so, I had adhered to another of the six steps in marketing—customer service. I guaranteed that the writing fit her immediate need as well as ensuring that the customer was happy with the product. My reward? In addition to full payment for the article, I received two more assignments from this editor over the next five months, and more will probably come.

Sounds simple, doesn't it? If it were always as easy as that, naturally, we would all be best-selling authors. It takes a great deal of undercover work to successfully fill the needs of most editors—for there are times when even they do not know what they need or want. Even before you start, however, you must ask yourself: "What do I have to offer?" There may be times when your answer is "nothing"—and there is no shame in that. You must simply move on to other markets.

What Do You Have to Offer?

Let me give you an example. Let's say you are a travel writer and have had three articles published—two in local newspapers and one in a national magazine. You would almost sell your first-born son to see your byline in *Travel and Leisure*. You even have a friend who works as a secretary to the managing editor. From her you've learned that, during the next thirteen months, the only editorial need is for foreign destination features, and the editors insist that writers have first-hand knowledge. Because a trip to Bali, Cairo, or Florence is not planned for your near future, you may be better off seeking markets with a wider opportunity, whereby you can fill an immediate need with your talents.

Another question that goes hand in hand with "What do I have to offer?" is "Who am I?" As strange as this may sound, rarely do we sit down and contemplate who we are and what we can provide an editor that no one else can. Have you ever done it?

Before you can successfully explore the needs of editors, and fill them, you first must know your own strong and weak points—and now is the time to find out. Sit down with a pen and paper. At the top of the page write: Who am I? Halfway down the page write: What do I have to offer? Then begin to make your list.

Here is mine:

Who Am I?
Male
Forty-five years old
American
Writer
Photographer
Married, with two children
BA in History/Government
Living in southern Italy
Four years in U.S. Navy
Hobbies: scuba diving, hiking

What do I have to offer?
Experience with U.S. military
Firsthand insight into Italy
Cross-cultural marriage
Raising children in a foreign country
Photographs with my features
An American view of European issues
Diving off the coast of Italy
Hiking the Alps
A love for Italian wines

The list could go on and on, but I think you've gotten the idea. Everyone—*EVERYONE*—has something to offer the right editor. When *Newsweek*'s special supplements editor,

Mark Svenvold, was looking for someone to write a feature on Italian fashions, a fellow member of the International Food, Wine and Travel Writers Association suggested he contact me. Why? Not because I am an expert on Italian fashions—I know very little about haute couture, in fact—but because I am (1) in Italy and (2) an American writer. In short, I filled the need with what I had to offer and who I was.

Based on your own lists, you should see a pattern of where you might best focus your marketing efforts. Let's say you've lived your entire life in Fort Worth, Texas. In an editor's eyes, this instantly makes you an expert on the city, the people, the history, the cowboy culture, even the rodeo and Billy Bob's Texas! You have, in your own backyard, hundreds of article and book ideas waiting to be discovered, explored, and written.

Just as I did not tell Mark Svenvold that I knew little about Italian fashions, there is no need for you to explain to an editor that you've never ridden a horse. Nor must you reveal that your only rodeo experience is what your Daddy used to watch on TV, and that while your girlfriends were at Billy Bob's looking for future husbands, you were getting a Ph.D. at Texas Tech. Selective revelations to editors is merely another aspect of marketing—sort of like the television ads telling you that the price has been slashed 20 percent, without saying the new bottle design also contains 20 percent less product.

I believe that a good, professional writer can write about anything. Therefore, when an editor offers me a job—whether it be about Italian fashions, underwater archaeology, protecting NATO's southern flank, or how to become a Latin Lover (yes, I did write that)—I rarely, if ever, say no. My research and interview skills are sufficient for me to put together an editorial package that is rarely refused. Yours should be too.

Once you have a good understanding of what ideas you can best market, based on your unique situation and skills, the real fun begins. If this were an army maneuver, now would be the time to select a target (a publication, a book publisher, or another niche). Next, an intelligence team would gather data and insight into the enemy (inside information regarding an editor's needs). Finally, soldiers would move in for the attack (your presentation). In your case, a victory means you've made a sale. Follow-up assignments might be considered a total massacre.

Assuming that you know the basics of locating a prime target for your work, whether an article or a book, let's concentrate on learning the needs of an editor—practicing undercover work. Traditionally, writers have turned to publications such as the annual *Writer's Market* or the monthly *Writer's Digest* magazine for leads. While these are both excellent resources for addresses and general information, there are two problems with limiting yourself to these references. First, because books normally require a year or more lead time to write and produce, the information found there is generally outdated. Second, when you read about a market in magazines like *The Writer, Writers' Journal,* or *Writer's Digest,* thousands of others are also reading the same material and submitting ideas and articles to those markets. As a result, editors are flooded with material and yours becomes lost in the swelling waters.

The Advertising Department

Your approach should be nontraditional. Go where others are not. Use guerrilla marketing to uncover the needs of editors who will be eager to receive your ideas, rather than those seeking only to stop the uncontrollable surge of submissions from writers. In the case of a magazine or newspaper, your first stop should be the advertising department.

Despite what editorial, production, and distribution people may tell you, it is the advertising folks who keep the cash flowing, keep the staff fed, and keep the publication in existence.

Newsstand and subscription sales of a magazine or newspaper rarely amount to much revenue in the overall scheme of publishing. Advertising, on the other hand, can make a publisher rich or send him to the poorhouse. In recent years, for example, top magazines like *People, Sports Illustrated, Parade, Time, TV Guide,* and *Newsweek* have enjoyed annual advertising revenues ranging from $384 million to $526 million. That is not a combined figure but, rather, per-publication revenue. Another example is *Better Homes & Gardens,* which, according to *Advertising Age,* recently posted annual ad revenues of $335 million.

Advertising people, because of the revenue they generate, generally have a tight hold on the reins of power. Their departments are better staffed than editorial offices. They reply almost immediately to all queries—since they never know where the next advertising dollars may come from. And they also freely give and distribute information that, in other departments, may be considered privileged. For example, annual editorial schedules.

By writing or calling a publication's advertising department and asking for the latest media kit (sometimes referred to as an advertising kit), you will normally be overwhelmed with data. These kits generally contain five things:

1. readership demographics
2. circulation information
3. reviews and general information about the magazine or newspaper
4. a sample copy
5. an editorial calendar and information on any special editions

While the readership data will help you better focus your queries, it is the editorial schedule that you really want.

Knowing what topics have already been approved and scheduled to run in the publication will allow you to focus your ideas on ways to specifically fill these needs. Keep in mind, however, that most magazines have a four- to twelve-month lead-time. Don't spend time proposing stories that would need to appear in two or three months. Begin at least six months ahead.

If you are asking yourself why an advertising department would send you—a freelance writer—a media kit, you need to go back and review the section about being a business. If you approach the ad reps as a writer, most likely they will *not* send you one. On the other hand, if a *business* asks for a media kit, it often goes out the next day. This is another example of why I suggest that you operate under a company name, rather than your own.

How do I know these things? Besides asking for current media kits from over twenty publications each year, I worked as an editor-advertising manager during the late 1980s for *R&R Magazine*, published in Germany. Wearing my editorial hat, I was always under tight budget constraints, never used courier service, and rarely made international calls. Changing to my advertising identity, I consistently called clients throughout Europe, sent tons of media kits by courier and express mail, and immediately followed up requests for information from potential advertisers.

I prefer to contact advertising departments by letter or e-mail rather than by phone, though either will work. My approach is straightforward and most often the letter is addressed to the advertising manager listed on the masthead of the publication. A normal pitch is:

As one of today's fastest growing editorial-marketing agencies, we (always use the plural, as it indicates a large business rather than a one-person operation) are exploring potential advertising venues for our customers. One or more clients have indicated interest in your publication. If you could provide a current media kit, including your advertising rates and long-term editorial schedule, it will better allow us to evaluate your magazine/newspaper in light of our customer's needs.

The most important point is that I specifically ask for the editorial calendar in the letter or the phone conversation. Using this method to gain inside information, I have sold hundreds of articles. In one case, with *Off Duty Publications,* I discovered that the editors were planning a special supplemental guide to the Mediterranean—my backyard—in the upcoming year. Armed with this information, I queried the editor of *Off Duty Europe* for a feature on Naples, Italy, one of the cities noted under the project. At the end of the letter, I added: "I look forward to hearing from you regarding this idea, or if you need other editorial material (articles and/or photographs) from the Mediterranean region."

A week later, editor Bruce Thorstad called to ask if I would consider being a contributing editor to their *Welcome to the Med Guide.* This translated into a solid job: providing all the text and photographs for the special edition. *Off Duty* put out the guide for three consecutive years and each time the publication contracted my services. Ultimately, lack of advertising killed the guide. So, ironically, the advertising department was responsible for both my landing and losing this job.

Angela Adair, editor and publisher of the Internet newsletter *National Writer's Monthly* and the *Write Markets Report, www.writersmarkets.com,* suggests that writers with the capability also search the Internet for guidelines and editorial calendars. Using one of the many popular Net search engines (AltaVista, Lycos, Hotbot, Mamma, and the like), Adair recently sought out current editorial calendars. The results were 378 matches.

"Most publications post their editorial calendar for advertisers," explains Angela. "But we writers can take advantage of this information as well."

To subscribe to *National Writer's Monthly,* send an e-mail message to *aadair@WritersMarkets.com* with "subscribe wm (your e-mail address)" in the subject header. This is a free e-mail newsletter.

Whether you are trying to sell an article or a book, or break into business media, inside contacts can be the key that opens the door to success. Those directly involved in corporate projects and editorial decisions know, before anyone else does, what the needs of a business are. My recent work for the Discovery Channel, for example, initially came about as a result of information from John Buffalo, a long-time friend and senior manager of corporate communications (I was best man at his wedding).

There are hundreds of individuals, besides editors, who have day-to-day insight into the editorial requirements of a company. Secretaries, advertising personnel, production and distribution managers, art directors, and even literary agents frequently know *years* ahead of time what a publishing house is up to. In a sense, these individuals can become your eyes and ears into industry needs.

While I am intentionally trying to avoid the word "spies," that, in the scheme of guerrilla marketing, is exactly what these contacts might be considered. The term I prefer, however, is "informants."

There is a catchphrase in the military called "OpSec," short for Operation Security. It was discovered during World

War II that the enemy was picking up much of its intelligence information in bars, where U.S. service members would go to drink and dance. While at a nearby table and sometimes even at the same table, enemy agents would chitchat with American GIs. During their discussion, soldiers would ultimately reveal such things as "the troops are pulling out next week" and "I'd better get my fill of booze because it will be four weeks before I get another opportunity."

Unknown to the soldiers, they had told the enemy agent—often an attractive, young female—that American units would be on the move for one month. This information, in turn, allowed the opposing forces to calculate which routes were more likely to be taken and what potential targets were within a thirty-day range; they were then able to establish the proper counterattack measures.

Today's troops are therefore warned to keep OpSec in mind at all times, particularly when in a foreign country—and in bars where good-looking women abound.

Because most people do not utilize OpSec tactics, you might easily get inside information into editorial needs over a cup of coffee, a dinner, during writers' conferences, or anywhere else publishing and corporate people gather. Not that editorial information is necessarily secret. Some editors will openly provide you with information for the asking. What you are seeking is company trends. Perhaps a new magazine is going to be launched by ABC Publications. More often than not, by the time a writer learns of this via traditional means, all the contributing editor and columnist slots are filled. If you knew someone at the company who informed you about the new magazine a year in advance, however, you could find out who the project decision maker was and propose yourself for such positions.

In 1985, while corresponding with Anne Crawford, then travel columnist for *Family Magazine,* I picked up from one of her letters that, "I'll be leaving the magazine next year to concentrate on book publishing." I immediately recognized an open door. After confirming with Anne that she had notified the magazine, I proposed myself, both to her and to Mary Jane Ryan, the editor-in-chief, to fill the vacancy. Anne supported the idea which, in turn, convinced Mary Jane to go along. Eventually, I not only wrote the monthly "At Ease" column, but produced all the travel features as well. This resulted in a nice monthly income as well as numerous complimentary vacations.

There are two very valuable points made by this illustration: (1) one must constantly be looking for a need to fill, and (2) the importance of networking cannot be underestimated. If you are not looking for open doors, you certainly will not find them. It would have been very easy for me to have read Anne's letter and simply moved on. So always, *ALWAYS* keep an eye open for potential needs by editors.

Be a Network Nut

I cannot say enough about the value of networking. I have had more work—and better-paying jobs—come my way through acquaintances, friends, and colleagues than from most traditional methods. There was a time when those geographically located in New York City and Los Angeles had a distinct advantage over the writer in, say, Backwater, Wyoming. They were able to establish a thick network of contacts from which to draw industrial information. Fortunately, with the invention of e-mail, this is no longer the case. In fact, if I can do it from Naples, Italy, so can you!

Like a good politician, a writer who knows how to establish and utilize a network is destined to succeed. Being a joiner is your first step. During my writing career, I have been a member of the American Society of Journalists and Authors; the International Food, Wine and Travel Writers

Association; the National Writers Association; the Travel Journalists Guild; and a horror writers group of which I can't even remember the name. Then there are the Publishers Marketing Association, the Small Press Association of North America, the International Association of Independent Publishers known as COSMEP, and several others. There were a number of reasons for joining each of these organizations. Expanding my network of colleagues was without a doubt one of the primary motivations.

Every group I am affiliated with provides a publication packed with industry news. These groups also offer directories of members and other beneficial services and information. What you do with these resources and data will determine the extent of the benefit you derive from them. Take, for example, the American Society of Journalists and Authors (ASJA). The society's monthly newsletter has provided leads to both editors and agents—though some writers may not immediately see this. Each issue includes lists of upcoming events, guest speakers slated to appear at Society events, and insights into the publishing industry. When I was seeking a new agent, I noted a feature article in which the author interviewed five active literary representatives. Noting what type of material each said they sought, I was able to target an agent perfect for my work.

On other occasions, the newsletter has reported comments by editors attending recent ASJA meetings or conferences. By tracking these comments, I have been able to locate editors who were seeking the type of material I was writing. This has led to several sales and, perhaps—it is currently in the second phase of consideration—placement of a nonfiction book idea.

Fellow members, no matter what the group, are perhaps the greatest of all benefits. When you attend functions of your organization, mix and mingle with others. Get to know as many people as possible. I recall one press trip, in particular, organized by the Philippine Tourist Board for members of the Travel Journalists Guild. Among those attending the ten-day event were Bob Milne, publisher of *TravelWriters Marketletter* (see the appendix), travel writer Alice Garrard, photographer/writer F. Lisa Beebe, as well as freelance photographer Rhonda Bishop. After days of skin-burning sun, tropical rains, and trekking through the jungles of Palawan, we'd established a bond. Bob would eventually talk me into publishing the *Markets Abroad* newsletter, which I did for eight years prior to the publication of my book, *The Writer's and Photographer's Guide to Global Markets*. Alice has since gone on to work for the Walt Disney Company, though we still stay in touch. Not long after the trip, I passed a lead onto Lisa Beebe that eventually landed her a contributing editor position with *R&R Magazine*. Rhonda Bishop and I collaborated on a couple of editorial packages, including a feature on jewelry for Philippine Airlines' in-flight magazine, *Mabuhay*.

This example illustrates how writers can benefit by sharing information and maintaining contact with colleagues. Following a meeting of the ASJA, the president of Tape Guide, Inc. approached veteran writer Bern Keating. Tape Guide was seeking writers to work on a project in Rome. During the conversation, Bern mentioned me. Two months later, we were both sitting outside a café in Piazza Venezia, sipping a fine Pallavicini white wine from Frascati and discussing our $1,500 assignments—plus expenses, of course. Considering the company had flown Bern from the United States to Rome, I believe he got the better of the two deals.

Clubs and associations offer an easy means of establishing a writer's network. It is up to you to take advantage of these. The appendix in the back of this book lists a couple of groups that can be beneficial to all writers. If nothing else, it is a place to begin.

Don't limit your networking to writers. Reach out, whenever possible, and rub elbows with publishers, editors, agents, and anyone else connected in some way to any paying market. Several years ago, as often happens, a colleague introduced me to Andria Lazis-Valentini, director of Articles International, a syndication business based in Canada. Following months of sharing information, Andria called to say that she'd been speaking with the editor of *Jake* magazine, published in New Mexico, and that he was looking for unique European ideas. I eventually sold him a piece on Italy's after-midnight sexual home shopping networks.

By maintaining contact with Articles International, and willingly offering insight into global markets, I prompted Lazis-Valentini to exchange the favor with the *Jake* assignment. Such sharing of information is common among today's best-paid writers.

"After a decade or two of writing for publication, so many journalists fall away into PR and other corporate work," says ASJA member Mary Mihaly. "I use those old colleagues as resources; one former city magazine editor now edits publications for Jones, Day, Reavis & Pogue (a mega-law firm, based in Cleveland) and she gives me four or five interesting assignments a year. Another friend now works solo as a PR person; she subcontracts a bimonthly newsletter to me that goes to clients of an insurance consultant. Another friend referred me to a psychiatry practice—for writing, not treatment. Another friend, a housing consultant, just hired me to pitch his newspaper column."

Through networking, Mary has been successful in uncovering the needs of corporate and business clients, then filling those needs. But her efforts do not stop there.

"Hand in hand with corporate work," she explains, "is nonprofit work. . . . I collect decent hourly fees writing for nonprofits, including hospitals, libraries, and organizations such as Ronald McDonald House. It's all interesting and enriching work, and a break from dealing with faceless editors long distance."

Nothing, since the days of jungle drums, has done more to enhance and ease one's ability to network as the Internet. However, establishing a good network takes time and energy, as Skip Press, Net guru and author of *Writer's Guide to Hollywood Producers, Directors and Screenwriter's Agents*, points out:

"Networking isn't an overnight thing. If you're just beginning as a writer, you need to find a local workshop group. If that's impossible geographically, then you need to find one online. Even then, it will take some time for people to get to know you, and you'll have to prove the worth of your writing and/or your ability to provide work and contacts for others."

As an example of the share-and-share-alike system to which Skip refers, here are a series of e-mail exchanges within our own online network.

- Skip Press, in Los Angeles, passed a message to me, introducing Jeremy Josephs, in Paris. Jeremy is seeking advice on selling and reselling articles; something in which I specialize. I, at the same time, am looking for contacts in the U.K. book publishing industry. Jeremy is English and has several books to his credit. Skip saw this as a perfect match.
- Eventually, I turned Josephs on to several editors around the world as well as an international syndication outfit. He has been selling to most of them since.
- Not long after that, Jeremy passed me a note saying that the editor of *Diplomat* magazine in London was looking for a contributor in Italy. I now fill that spot.

- After the publication of my first book with Allworth Press, I noted that they also have a line of titles for the performing arts. I therefore suggested that Skip query them with a Hollywood-theme book. He did so and, as a result, has landed a contract with the publisher.
- Two weeks later, Press informed me that the online magazine *Internet.com* was seeking European correspondents. Within twenty-four hours, I had contacted Editor-in-chief Gus Venditto. I now provide *Internet.com* with two articles a month.

This exchange of e-mail messages shows just how a good, strong network of writers can help one another. It also places emphasis on the sharing of information.

"My rule has always been to share every contact I have with anyone for whom I think the connection would be mutually beneficial," continues Skip Press, who is known among his Internet contacts as "the Duke of URLs" (the latter term, if you do not know, refers to the unique routing locator, or address, of sites on the World Wide Web). "The emphasis is on *mutual.* Most writers do not do this, frankly, nor do most people, at least not in my experience. I have found that most people protect their contacts and are very reluctant to share them."

Participating in Internet newsgroups like alt.writing, misc.writing, misc.writing.screenplays, or alt.journlism is one way to establish contacts. Too often, however, joining such groups is like throwing your time and effort to the wind. A much better way to contribute and receive professional advice and contacts is to join list discussions. As opposed to newsgroups, discussion groups are more like closely linked clubs. In addition, replies come by way of e-mail messages, either directly to you or to the entire group.

One of my favorite discussion groups is that of the ASJA. It is open to all active members and you join through the Web site *www.onelist.com*. From this same site, you can join the Fiction Writers Forum, the Horror Forum, the Editor Forum, and a variety of other groups that will let you communicate and network with others.

This is not the only Web site offering discussion groups, however. There are hundreds. Computer book writers, for example, have StudioB at *www.studiob.com*. CompuServe offers a variety of newsgroups, discussion groups, and chat areas such as its screenwriting chat or misc.writing.screenplays. The CompuServe crowd, generally, has more serious writers and working professionals. To find a group that fits your particular writing interest, simply do a search of the Internet.

Book Publishing Insight

Guerrilla marketers know several ways to discover and fulfill the needs of book publishers. Networking, naturally, is one. You might have noted that I hold membership in several organizations for publishers. This is because I firmly believe that you must understand as much as possible about the book publishing industry if you intend to succeed in selling your work in this form. You must know what drives publishing houses, how large they are, how they distribute their titles, the number of titles they produce, how they print, and who their editors are. Then, and only then, will you be able to successfully fill the need of a particular publisher. For this reason, I expanded my "intelligence network" into the publishing sector several years ago.

> "I spend as long promoting a book as I do writing it. I only stop when I am so damned sick of the subject— which is why I write on different subjects for each book—that I can't do anything further on it."
>
> —*Paulette Cooper, author of eleven books, including* The Scandal of Scientology

Among the first things I learned was that a subscription to *Publisher's Weekly (www.bookwire.com/pw/pw.html)* was a must. Not only did it provide the most up-to-date information on the industry—rather than the long outdated references offered by some publishers—but it told me what editors were on the move, where they were going, where they'd been, and what their new position would entail. As a marketing warrior, I put this knowledge to work immediately.

During this period I was covering U.S. military and NATO affairs in the Mediterranean region for The Associated Press. I therefore came up with an idea for a book on NATO assault aircraft. Based on a special edition of *Publisher's Weekly,* which listed the fall book releases, I noted that Arco Press specialized in such titles. Calling the company, I was told the editor for this genre was Henry Rasof.

The next day a proposal was in the mail. Three weeks later, Rasof's rejection arrived. Over the next year I would propose four more books. All four would be rejected. While flipping the pages of a later *Publisher's Weekly,* I noted under editor movements that Rasof had gone to Franklin Watts to work in its children's division. Because I always have a few book ideas on the back burner, off went a letter with two book ideas to Henry, who by now had become almost a friend. This time, rather than a reject, he wrote: "I've never seen someone so persistent—even so as to follow me to a new publishing house. I'm not keen on your ideas, but let me give you one. We are looking for a writer to produce a book on the ocean for our Impact series . . ."

The following year, my book, *Commercialization of the Oceans,* was selected as a Best Book of the Year for its category by the New York Public Library system. I have *Publisher's Weekly,* Henry Rasof, and my persistent marketing to thank for this.

In addition to *Publisher's Weekly*, there are several other trade publications—*American Bookseller Magazine, Kirkus Reviews, Library Journal, Small Press Magazine, Book*—that can help you better focus your sales efforts. Joining the right publishers' associations will also get you monthly newsletters and membership directories that can frequently be valuable marketing tools.

Another successful method to gain insight into the specific needs of book publishers—one that writers, to my amazement, frequently overlook—is perusal of the annual sales catalogs these companies produce. They are free for the asking at any publishing house, and illustrate what editors are buying. Too often writers try to come up with new, unique trends and topics, when 80 percent of all publishers work specific niches. They don't want *new*. They don't want *trend*. What they want is something that will complement their current list, because that is what they know how to sell.

An excellent example of this is the book you now hold. I found Allworth Press not in *Writer's Market* or in popular writers' magazines, but in an association directory of small presses. I specifically went to this source because I knew few writers would—therefore limiting the competition. I then requested a copy of Allworth's current catalog. Once in my hands, I noted several titles on freelance writing and photography. One in particular was *The Photographer's Guide to Marketing and Self-Promotion*. I found it interesting, however, that there was not a similar title for writers. Upon querying the publisher—one of the benefits of small presses is that you can frequently go to the decision maker directly—I received a letter stating: "We've been considering such a book for some time, but have yet to find a writer. If you are interested, please send us a proposal. . . ."

Some writers today talk about the frustration of getting a book contract. One person recently told me that "It's like being a dog and chasing your own tail, day after day after day." I then asked, "When was the last time you attended a book fair?" He looked at me rather curiously and replied, "Why would I go to a book fair?"

Off the top of my head I could think of three reasons. First, to sell to an editor you must know the environment in which an editor works. Second, annual conventions like BookExpo America (formerly the American Booksellers Association convention) reveal the likes, dislikes, and needs of nearly every publisher in the United States and beyond. Third, there is no better place for networking with publishing people than a convention. I try to attend three book fairs a year. In addition to BookExpo, I like to make the Frankfurt International Book Fair and the London Book Fair. I bring a fresh box of 500 business cards and spend hours distributing and collecting cards of publishers, editors, and literary agents. I speak with those who have time, discuss their jobs, their products, and their plans for the future. Armed with this information, book ideas seem to blossom like wildflowers in an open meadow. Suddenly, I have "friends" rather than strangers to send my proposal to.

There are book conventions of all types held throughout the United States, and the world, each year. If you cannot attend the large fairs, at least make an attempt to visit a few local exhibitions. For dates and locations, I suggest *Publisher's Weekly* and *Book Marketing Update* (see the appendix), or *www.bookwire.com*.

I have always enjoyed meeting publishers, editors, and agents face to face. Perhaps it is because I feel they have so much to offer with regard to industry knowledge. Long ago, however, I learned that very rarely do these individuals willingly reveal their true needs, unless they are convinced of your professionalism or you present them with an idea that "hits the nail on the head." In both cases, premeeting planning—sometimes even covert operations—is required.

In most cases, setting up a meeting with a magazine or book editor is as easy as a phone call, particularly in the first case. The higher up you go in the corporate echelons, however, the less time individuals have for chitchat with potential writers. Meetings with editors in chief or publishers, therefore, often require tactical warfare.

First, know the individual's background. Did she come from another publishing house? What type of material does she like? Is she married? How many years has she been with the company? What's her ethnic background? Is she an animal lover? Is she involved in any social groups? Every detail you can pick up will help you meet with, and sell your work to, that particular person.

Using a method I discovered while researching a novel involving the Naval Investigative Services, I prepare a profile of the person I am about to meet. It's not as much work as it seems. In fact, it is about as easy as keeping an index file. Let's say, for example, you want to meet with John Beechman. You've learned from *Publisher's Weekly* that he is heading HarperCollins Publishers' new self-help imprint. But what else do you know about him?

- The magazine listing also said that he was previously a senior editor at HarperPrism, and the new position also promoted him to executive editor.
- Next, you do an Internet search and learn that Mr. Beechman was editor of several college textbooks and that prior to coming to HarperCollins, he worked for Franklin Watts.
- A visit to a library that collects textbooks reveals a biography, two years old, stating that "John Beechman was a professor of psychology at Grand Rapids Community College prior to becoming a writer and

editor. He now lives in New York City with his wife, Mary, and two children, Daniel and Kathy."

- You take some time to read a few passages from Beechman's edited works—taking notes and paying particular attention to any introductions that he specifically wrote. This gives you insight into his style, thinking, and personality. One thing you note is a strong undertone of spirituality.
- Next, you tap into your network of colleagues, editors, agents, and friends to see if any of them have ever had any dealings with Beechman. Jennifer Smart, a New York literary agent, sold him two books last year. From her you get: "He's a very intelligent family man—and religious." You then ask if she minds you using her name as an introduction. "No," she replies. "But don't be pushy."

The more data you acquire, the better your profile will be. With only the information above, you could put together an attractive introductory letter. First, however, decide when you want to establish the meeting. Always offer a span of days and times, say, Tuesday to Thursday, for lunch or in the early afternoon. Next, call Beechman's secretary, and ask if he will be in town and available during those periods.

When I do this, I go into role playing. The conversation normally goes something like this: "Good morning, this is David Jeffries of the Strawberry Media Agency. I'm calling on behalf of our director, Michael Sedge. He is interested in meeting with Mr. Beechman during his upcoming trip to New York. Will Mr. Beechman be available, say, next Tuesday through Thursday?"

In most cases, unless the boss has given free rein for appointment bookings, secretaries will not arbitrarily arrange a meeting. If the opportunity to confirm a meeting does arise in the conversation, great. Take it, but don't be pushy. Also, don't forget to get the secretary's name.

As I said previously, at smaller publications you can often go directly to the editor. At larger houses, try asking for the secretary. I have discovered that calling at lunch, when top executives are normally out, is a good time. And always make your "company" sound larger than life.

After you've confirmed that your "target" will be on the battlefield during your invasion, it's time for a prewarning letter. Simply gather your facts—from the profile card—and utilize your writing talents. I might produce something like the following:

Dear Mr. Beechman,

Congratulations on your recent advancement and new imprint—you've come a long way from Franklin Watts. I believe you were there during the same period as Henry Rasof, who edited my *Commercialization of the Oceans* for Watts's Impact series. I now head the Strawberry Media Agency in Naples, Italy, but maintain contact with Henry.

During a recent conversation with Jennifer Smart, I mentioned that I would soon be visiting New York City. She suggested that I meet with you to discuss two projects I am currently involved in—both based on spirituality and family.

My assistant spoke with your secretary, Diane Jacobs, yesterday to confirm that you would be in town Tuesday through Thursday. I specifically asked him not to book an appointment, however, until I first communicated with you. I've intentionally scheduled my meetings on those days during the mornings, leaving me free for lunch or an afternoon encounter. Lunch on Tuesday would be excellent for me. If you could have Ms. Jacobs advise us if this works for you, by

return fax or e-mail, I will be pleased to block sufficient time for an enjoyable meal.

I look forward to meeting you.

Sincerely,

Michael H. Sedge
Director
Strawberry Media, Inc.
Via Venezia 14/b
80021 Afragola (NA) Italy
Tel: (011) 39-081-851-2208
Fax: (011) 39-081-851-2210
E-mail: *Pp10013@cybernet.it*

*P.S. What years were you at Grand Rapids College? I lived in
Kentwood for nineteen years.*

Looking closely at the above letter, you'll see that I opened
with a compliment—a technique I stole from the Metro-
politan Life Insurance agent's manual. I also mentioned his
past editorial position with Franklin Watts—indicating I was
not a complete stranger to his background—and pointing
out that I had worked with a colleague at his previous company. This single line subconsciously tells Beechman that (1)
I am a published author, (2) I keep up with the publishing
industry, and (3) I know people in the industry.

In this same paragraph, I tell him who I am (head of
Strawberry Media, Inc.) and where I am located (Naples,
Italy). This is yet another example of how a company name
can be used as a "front" for writers—there will be many others in the chapters to come. Using a company name, I am
able to make myself the director, editor-in-chief, president,
or any title that fits the situation. My intent with Beechman
is to create questions in his mind, to stimulate his curiosity:
"What does the Strawberry Media Agency do? Is it an orga-

nization of literary agents? Is it a group of book packagers? Does it represent foreign publishers?" I do not, however, provide him with answers—one more reason for him to meet with me.

Listing where I am located and that I am traveling thousands of miles to meet him adds a sense of urgency to our meeting and, as well, illustrates the importance I place on our encounter. The reaction I want here is, "If he is coming from so far away, I can at least give him thirty minutes of my time." If you work from a small town, use the nearest major city when telling people where you are operating. This will add prestige to your business. For example, if you live in Black Hawk, Colorado, say that your operation is in Denver. If you're in Opa-locka, Florida, use Miami.

I then drop another name, that of Jennifer Smart. You'll recall that she sold Beechman two titles last year and, thus, hers is a good recommendation. He might subconsciously think, "If she suggested we meet, there must be something of value in his projects." Or at least that is what I hope he thinks. I also mention that my projects are based on spirituality (the theme of the new imprint) and the family (he is married with two children).

I continue that my assistant (suddenly I am not a one-man operation) spoke with Diane Jacobs (listing her name confirms the conversation). The simple fact that I have an assistant indicates that I am a busy man—perhaps as busy as Beechman. We, therefore, are on a level playing field. What you don't want to do, when dealing with upper-level managers, publishers, or editors, is come across as a freelance writer. In most cases, this would result in your being pushed onto a lower-level associate editor or even get you a negative reply to your request for a meeting.

Next comes the time frame in which I can meet. I first point out that I did not have my assistant book the meeting—a professional courtesy, allowing him to pick the time and place. He may very well decide to meet over lunch—I've offered this option—thus giving us more time as well as saving me the expense of a meal (he has an expense account for such things; writers do not).

I close by specifically asking that he have Ms. Jacobs reply by fax or e-mail. This calls for action on his part, a decision. If you leave an opening for an "escape," editors will frequently take it. Make them react to your letter.

Finally, I add the P.S. about his years at Grand Rapids Community College and point out that I, too, lived near there. This gives us one more element in common and something else to discuss at our get-together. It may be that he loved teaching and agrees to see me simply to talk about this period in his life. That's fine with me, as long as it gets me a fixed time and date to discuss what I want as well.

Some writers do a great job at opening doors to editors and other industry personnel but drop the ball when the actual meeting takes place. This is the time to become a salesperson, not a flounder out of water. You need not be pushy or even attempt to get an assignment or contract. Rather, use the encounter to pave the way for future work, to dig deeper into the client's needs, and to leave him with ideas.

If you have never worked with the publisher, editor, or corporate executive with whom you are meeting, always bring a press kit (discussed in chapter 7). You will want to ensure that the kit is slanted toward your prospective client's needs. For example, if you are trying to get work as a corporate speechwriter, you might include quotes from previous clients, samples of your work, and a price list. That's right, a price list. The business world is used to working in a certain way. This includes fixed prices for services, or estimates in advance. Invoices upon completion of the job, and payment within thirty or sixty days. By preparing a price list in advance, there will be no questions with regard to your fees, you will dictate the amount you receive rather than the client, and executives can more easily get jobs approved through the company accounting system.

If you've published books, copies of these should also be included, if appropriate. Above all else, however, bring ideas that fit what the potential customer needs. Your premeeting research into the company will establish what type of material you offer. If you have completed query letters—for magazine editors—bring them. If you are meeting a book editor, try to have at least one book proposal (for nonfiction) or a synopsis (in the case of fiction). If you have more than one idea, bring more—but don't overload the editor.

When I have enough information to know the likes and dislikes of various editors, I might also bring a token gift to the meeting. Knowing that *R&R Magazine* had recently moved into a new office building, I purchased a plant while on my way to see editor Tori Billard. On other occasions I have presented editors with calendars, pens, autographed books, and a variety of useful items. For people I have worked with, and know well, I might even bring a "special" bottle of Italian wine.

Remember that everything you do, including meetings and gifts, are part of the marketing process. The meeting is designed for you to listen, gather information, and present ideas. The gift, on the other hand, should have some marketing value, if possible. If you are giving a calendar, for example, be sure that it highlights your name, your company, and such information as mailing address, telephone, fax, and e-mail. While visiting an editor in Los Angeles, I noted the annual "Christmas present" calendar I had sent, hanging on the wall.

"Glad to see you put it to good use," I told her.

"Good use," she replied. "It is one of the most valuable things in the office. And when I need an article or photos, I simply glance up and have your numbers. Beats going through 500 business cards."

In this particular case, I had specifically selected a calendar that listed annual events—National Fitness Week, Black History Month, and so on. After my meeting, I sent the editor a letter suggesting an article on Alex Haley, author of the bestselling novel *Roots,* whom I had recently interviewed. As a close, I wrote, "If you'll go ahead a few months in the wall calendar, you'll note that Black History Month might be a perfect time for such a feature." That clinched the sale.

I always have a stash of pens and other inexpensive office items—Post-its, rulers, erasers, penholders, and so on—with my company name and information preprinted on them. This way, when it comes time to meet with potential clients, it is easy to slip a few into my briefcase.

Now what about that "special" wine? In this case I found a vineyard that would create a special label if I purchased a minimum of fifty bottles. I did, and received "Strawberry Media Wines. Bottled for the editor without energy, the publisher without pep, and the agent without aggression. For all your editorial needs, write, call, fax, or e-mail Strawberry Media . . . Then sit back, relax, and have a drink on us." This went over exceedingly well and, based on the work I received from the individuals who got a bottle of Strawberry Media special, it was a marketing success.

"I consider marketing crucial to my writing success. Over 50 percent of my time is spent on marketing efforts. In my opinion, most writers can manage the technical skills of their craft but do a poor job of marketing themselves and their work. One of the most important things

> that I do that pays in new writing assignments is to travel to my major markets—New York, Chicago, Florida, and California—on a regular basis to meet in person with current and prospective editors. This puts a face with the piece of paper they receive. As you develop a personal relationship, they turn to you for more work, providing you do a good job for them."
>
> *—Chris Maturi, author of fifteen books and over one thousand published articles*

I normally go into meetings with magazine editors with two printed copies of a prospective article list. This contains between five and ten story ideas, including possible titles and a short overview of the topic. Naturally, I have done as much undercover investigation as possible to know what the editor needs for future issues, and specifically tailored my ideas to these requirements. I have also taken the time to scan what has been published during the past three or four months. When the proper time arises, I bring out my lists, hand one to the editor, and say, "Here are a few ideas I'd like to go over with you, if you have the time. Otherwise I can just leave it." It is rare that I do not walk away with at least two assignments.

Meeting book editors and publishers sometimes calls for more listening than selling. Here is an excellent example of how I utilized networking not only to gain insight into industry personnel, but to get one foot into the door for face-to-face encounters. I had sent a book proposal to Ken Atchity, an agent in Beverly Hills. It was an idea about Italy, where Atchity, I learned in my research, had lived and taught for many years. Upon receipt, he passed it on to his executive editor, Monica Faulkner. In turn, she notified me that it was not for them, but that she had spoken with another agent, Toni Lopopolo, who was interested. I therefore authorized her to pass it on to Lopopolo. Eventually Toni and I met.

In my premeeting, undercover work, I discovered that Lopopolo was once a top fiction editor for St. Martin's Press and was still very much respected in New York literary circles. I also found out that she had moved from the Big Apple to California two years earlier, she had graduated from New York College, she had a love of dogs, and some other tidbits about her personal and professional life.

Because of our mutual love for Italy and the publishing industry, we hit it off immediately. Over a superb Italian meal, Lopopolo discussed book editors who also shared an interest in the Mediterranean peninsula—I took note of each one. Having been in publishing for many years, Toni shared some of her experiences. All of this gave me greater insight into writers, editors, publishers, and agents—allowing me to create profiles of each individual.

At one point—I think it was when the espresso arrived—I mentioned a book idea about a dog that I was contemplating. Knowing she loved dogs and had two of her own, I was not surprised when she perked up. Then again, it may have just been the coffee.

"Do you know any editors who might be interested?"

"Dog lovers? There are lots in the editing business. Try Maureen O'Neal at Ballantine. And Heather Jackson at St. Martin's Press, Susan Kamil at Dell. Then there is Tom Dunne, who has his own imprint. In fact, Dunne used his dachshund as the company logo."

I came away from our meeting with a wealth of information and insight into various book editors and publishers. In addition, I ensured that she would not mind me using her name when approaching these individuals. This provided an added benefit, since most of the people we discussed were personal friends—and editors, in my experience, look more closely at a project if it's recommended by a friend and, in this case, a past editor and agent.

In addition to opening a dialogue with each of the editors Lopopolo had mentioned, I discovered that Tom Dunne was coming to Italy for a one-week vacation. Because of my experience in and his passion for the country, I offered my services as a guide for a day—which he gladly accepted. In doing this, I had ensured myself perhaps five hours with a veteran publisher who produces roughly 150 titles a year; including the works of Rosamunde Pilcher and Wilbur Smith. So busy is Dunne in New York that you can rarely reach him by phone, let alone arrange a meeting.

Ultimately, the encounter with Tom and his wife, Mary, lasted ten hours, and ended with drinks at their Sorrento hotel. We shared insights into the publishing industry, he provided tips on titles for a couple of my projects, and when he said he would be glad to review my work, I presented him with two folders, each containing a nonfiction book proposal. No pressure, no sales pitch. We met on neutral ground, as equals. When we departed, I realized that I had a new, influential friend in the New York publishing industry.

What did I learn about Dunne's needs? In his own words: "Every editor, every publisher needs to put out a given number of books each year. Writers must fill this requirement. What do editors want? In most cases, they don't really know until they've seen it."

The Phone Call

In your efforts to discover a client's needs, if all else fails, pick up the phone. While some writers will disagree with this tactic, I have found it very successful. When I cannot get through to the editor, I normally attempt to befriend the secretary. In a few cases, I have even gone so far as to query the secretary rather than the editor. Here is how one encounter went:

"*Woman Today* magazine, may I help you?"

"Good morning. I'd like to speak with Lea Thompson, please."

"I'm sorry, Ms. Thompson is in a meeting."

To which I replied: "May I ask who I am speaking with?"

"This is Jennifer Knight, Lea's secretary."

"Hi, Jennifer. This is Michael Sedge calling from Italy."

"From Italy! I just love that country."

(The door just opened wide.)

"You've been here?"

"Oh, yes, twice. Where exactly are you located?"

"In Naples. I'm, you might say, in the shade of Vesuvius."

"You must love it. What can I do for you?"

(Now comes my pitch, using the knowledge I've just gained.)

"Since you've been to Italy twice, Jennifer, you've probably heard that Italians are supposedly great 'Latin Lovers.' I just wanted to ask Lea if she'd be interested in an article based on that theme, say, how to turn your man into a Latin Lover. And, if she is interested, would she mind my sending a query by fax."

"Well," said Jennifer, "it sure sounds interesting to me! And we get fax queries all the time from our regular contributors."

"That's great. I'll just fax in a query then. Thanks for your help, Jennifer . . . and if you need anything from Italy, give me a call."

"Thank you, Mr. Sedge. Goodbye."

I then proceeded to prepare a query letter NOT addressed to Thompson, but to Jennifer. In our three-minute conversation I had found a common bond between us—Italy. I opened the letter with:

Dear Jennifer,

It was a pleasure talking with you today—and I was serious about helping with anything you might need from Italy. If you could pass the query below to Ms. Thompson, I would be grateful.

For the most part, secretaries lead very busy, yet unglamorous lives. At the same time, their bosses are frequently in the spotlight. Showering them with attention, I have often made inroads that I would never have made otherwise. In the case of Jennifer, I later learned that she personally took the query to her boss, telling her what an interesting idea I'd proposed for a feature. It was also Jennifer who ultimately called with the assignment.

At Christmas—and after receiving payment for my published article—I sent her a thank-you note along with a locally produced ceramic flower. You would have thought I had given her a new Volvo. She called with joy and thanks. Needless to say, whenever I need information from *Woman Today*, it is only a phone call away.

"When I am down to two or three magazine assignments, I start calling the various editors I know and pitch ideas to them. It's crucial to do this well ahead of time, since editors can be very slow while your idea endlessly circulates."

—Lisa Collier Cool, author of Bad Boys

But what happens when you do get through to the editor? How do you get information then? First, you must never, ever call an editor with a vague idea or no idea at all. These are busy people with very little time or patience for nonproductive discussions. When I was an editor, I was happy to receive serious calls. If a writer asked, "How much do you pay?" or "I'm going to England, would you like an article?" I had to control myself not to hang up.

A professional writer should have done enough homework to know the general types of articles an editor uses. He should know what the rates are, along with article lengths and styles. And, most important, the writer should have a very focused concept of what the article will be about. Here are a couple of successful examples.

> "Michele Babineau."
>
> "Good morning, Michele. This is Michael Sedge, director of the Strawberry Media Agency. . . .
>
> *(Note that I do not introduce myself as a writer, but use the company as a front.)*
>
> . . . I've just gotten off the phone with the director of Cross-Country International, a company that offers horseback stag hunting vacations south of Paris. This sounded like a perfect activity for your readership and, since I will be in Paris next week, I'd like to propose an exclusive feature for *Robb Report.*"
>
> *(Note the key word:* exclusive. *In this news-possessed world, everyone wants exclusivity.)*
>
> "It does sound right for us," she said.
>
> "Why don't I fax you a query?" I said. "This will allow me to include my credentials. I might add that I can also provide photographs."
>
> *(Always give customers* more *than they expect, if possible.)*

Six months later "To the Hunt" appeared in the pages of *Robb Report* and I was $800 richer.

Another good example occurred recently when I called *Diplomat,* a bimonthly magazine published in the United Kingdom. The conversation went like this:

> "This is Michael Sedge, director of Strawberry Media in Italy. I've recently been granted an interview with

Admiral T. Joseph Lopez, commander in chief of Allied Forces Southern Europe, and I wonder if you would be interested in exclusive rights to this feature."

"It's hard to say without knowing a little more about the admiral," said editor Mark Cockle.

I replied, "I can fax or e-mail you additional information if you'd like. If you could then let me know your decision by the end of the week, that would be sufficient."

"E-mail will work fine . . . "

The article, "Four Star Peacekeeper," appeared in *Diplomat* the following September.

The key to these telephone success stories is that, first, I was offering articles that practically no one else could, and such pieces had not appeared in that or any competing publication. Second, I was providing "exclusivity" (although in each case the magazines only got exclusive, first serial rights for the country in which they were published—because they preferred not to pay the high price I asked for world rights). This second factor justified a call rather than a letter.

What the calls really boiled down to, though, was whether or not the editors needed such articles. Once that was confirmed, I immediately reverted to offering a written query. This made them comfortable and gave them an opportunity to discover who I was and what I had to offer. It also gave them the option to say no.

The advice and examples of this chapter illustrate one thing: You must find out the specific needs of potential clients. There are numerous ways of discovering this information. Those who get ahead and make the big money are, for the most part, writers who use a combination of these methods. They utilize nontraditional sources to figure out the requirements of editors, publishers, and corporate clients. From advertising kits and inside informants to global networking and covert operations, you must be a guerrilla marketer if you are to win at the writing game. Knowing the needs of potential clients is 50 percent of the battle. Armed with this information, you can then focus on the attack—that is, presenting your products and services.

PRODUCT STRATEGY

When people ask me what I do, I rarely, if ever, say that I am a freelance writer. More often, my answer is, "I operate an international editorial services agency." Sounds impressive, doesn't it? Sounds, almost as if I single-handedly operate The Associated Press or United Press International. At this point, particularly at parties and other gatherings, someone will undoubtedly ask, "Exactly what is that?"

"I provide editorial packages—articles, photographs, books, speeches, and the like—to approximately forty customers around the world" is my standard reply.

This type of conversation is what I refer to as "business talk." And, as the old saying goes, if you are going to walk the walk, you've got to talk the talk. Exactly what walk you walk and what talk you talk is going to determine the category into which potential customers classify you. If, for example, you talk "service," "product," and "presentation," they will recognize these as marketing buzzwords, thus making you a "business" person. On the other hand, if terms such as "freelance," "query," and "self-addressed, stamped envelope" are common in your vocabulary, you may find yourself placed in the "person who writes for a hobby" or "artist" classification. For this reason—and despite any creative-writing courses you may have taken—you must first think marketing and then writing. It's the guerrilla way of doing business, and will ensure your success. As a writer, you have a double-edged sword to use on potential buyers. Whereas most companies sell either "services" or "products," you can offer both. In fact, you even have a third option.

In the service category, first of all, you are a writer for hire. Clients have a need for a writer and they contact you. After completing the job, you provide an invoice and collect your fee. Second, you provide—after a sales presentation (query letter, book proposal)—completed products in the form of articles, books, and so on. The third option is *you*. Yes, you too are a product.

The Market Environment

Before you can establish a successful marketing campaign, you must first fully understand the market environment in which you work as well as the services and products you offer. What is the competition? How do your services and products differ from the competition? How can you make them more attractive to potential buyers? These are the questions you must answer for each sector of your business.

Let's begin by looking at your "service" as a writer. Unlike the traditional method of doing business, whereby

you come up with ideas and query editors or media directors—in the case of corporate work—this segment of your
operation consists of potential customers calling you when
they need . . . what? That's right. Your "service."

Your writing service will develop naturally as you sell
more and more work to a variety of clients. This may take
years, however. Fortunately you do not have to—and
should not—follow the slow-moving, name recognition path
that most writers do. Why? First, because clients that call for
writing services normally pay more. Second, because these
customers often come from the ranks of top-name publications and corporations.

As an example, in 1982, the editor-in-chief of
BankAmerica *World,* the company's in-house magazine,
called me. The magazine needed a writer in my geographical
area to produce a thousand-word feature on a local bank.
The fee was $1 a word, paid on completion.

How did he get my name? I had prepared a brochure
one year before and mailed it to three hundred corporate
media managers.

"One of the best ways to start getting corporate work
is to attend meetings and events sponsored by the
International Association of Business Communications (IABC). There are chapters in most major cities
around the world. Most members are people on staff
in corporate communications, public relations, and
marketing departments who are often looking for freelance help. Local chapters are usually listed in the
business white pages."

—*Jack El-Hai, writer*

Other examples of top-paying work that has come my way
from clients requiring a writer's service include: Franklin

Watts ($4,200), H&R Block ($5,000), Holiday Inn ($3,200), *Newsweek International* ($1,000), Rapid Link Telecommunications ($1,870), Tape Guide, Inc. ($1,500), the Discovery Channel ($14,000), Time-Life ($1,200), U.S. Navy ($1,500), and the United Service Organization (USO) ($12,000). As you can see, it pays to dedicate time and effort to developing and building service customers. Later, when we get into your market approach, we'll dig deeper into reaching these potential clients and informing them about your services.

There are three reasons a client would typically request your services: (1) you live in a specific geographical area or have an expertise in a particular field; (2) his deadline is too tight for a staff writer or regular contributor to do the job; (3) he normally does not work with writers but, in this particular case, needs a "word mechanic." Therefore, it makes sense for you to concentrate on these areas in your marketing. For instance, perhaps you live in Orlando. This makes you the perfect candidate for anyone seeking an article on Walt Disney World (geographical expertise), Sea World, and an array of other attractions in the city. On the other hand, suppose you have worked, as I have, in the telecommunications field. You no doubt have a better understanding of (expertise in) this industry than most writers do. This makes you a good choice to fulfill the writing needs—marketing, advertising, and corporate communications—of the numerous communications companies across the country.

If you can write quickly and accurately, you're a valued asset to clients under tight deadlines. This sometimes means dropping everything else and working into the early morning hours to accomplish the desired task. However, this type of dedication, in my experience, can pay off big time.

Expanding Your Services

In December of 1980, I received a call from James Kitfield, editor of *Overseas Life* magazine, published in Germany. Mount Etna had come to life the previous week, belching molten lava into the Sicilian skyline, and Kitfield, knowing I live in southern Italy, called to ask if I could have a feature about the erupting volcano written and to him within three days.

"If you can also include great photos," he continued, "there's a chance it could be our cover story."

My mind was reeling. The story deadline was not a problem, but where would I get the images? Fortunately, the local media grapevine turned up Robert Zehring, a retired air force colonel and ex-NASA public affairs officer. With a passion for live volcanoes, Zehring had spent the past forty-eight hours tiptoeing up the slopes of Etna and was able to provide spectacular images. Thanks to his talents as a lensman and my ability to produce a feature on demand, we landed the February 1981 cover with "Hot Foot Adventures."

We split the profits, by the way.

This experience got me thinking about the service I offered. Up to that point I had been a writer, like thousands of others, offering a pen for hire. I now realized that this was not enough. By expanding my services to include photographs, I would not only set myself apart from the crowd, but also increase my income. The next day I called Zehring, who had a stock of nearly 500,000 slides. A week later we signed a contract under which I would become a broker for his images. Over the next ten years, the bylines of Sedge and Zehring would appear in hundreds of periodicals around the world—mine on the articles, his on the images. I was collecting 100 percent of the profits for the writing and 40 percent of the photo income.

"Employ photography. Dramatic pictures will sell a story more quickly than anything you can do."

—*Downs Matthews, professional writer*

Requests for my writing increased because editors knew that I could provide text/photo packages. What we had set up, basically, was one-stop shopping for editors. Whereas shoppers once went to individual stores for meat, bread, and other staples, they now go to a major supermarket and get everything they need—saving both time and money. We had simply applied this concept to the media business. Under our arrangement, editors no longer needed to shop around.

Soon art directors were also calling me with image needs. By 1990 my service operation had expanded to the point that I was representing fourteen photographers around the world and filling more than ten requests for pictures and articles each month—including such customers as The Associated Press, *Newsweek, Travel-Holiday,* and Time-Life Books.

By incorporating photography, my writing business boomed. The enhancement of my services, however, did not stop there. For years, I had worked with local printers for my company stationery, business cards, presentation folders, and other needs.

It occurred to me, while talking with the administrative director of the University of Maryland, that nearly every school, company, and organization required writers, photographers, and printers to produce their books, catalogs, brochures, and promotional materials. So, as I had done with Bob Zehring ten years before, I was soon signing contracts with local printers to receive a 15 percent commission on all jobs I brought them.

Less than a week later I was writing, providing the photos, and handling the printing of an eight-page, full-color brochure for the USO Mediterranean Headquarters. My profit, after paying all expenses, would be $7,000.

By getting away from the stigma of a "freelance writer" and expanding my services to include photography and printing, my business jumped light-years ahead of the competition. My phone, fax, and now e-mail are constantly active with requests. This should also be your goal. It is not that hard to achieve if you consistently provide fast, professional-quality products and always look for opportunities to expand your services.

Your Products

While you, as a writer, provide a service, your business also offers products. For the most part, these are the articles and books you produce. Unlike a service job, whereby a client calls you, it is your job to approach and sell your products to potential buyers. We have already discussed a few guerrilla methods to enhance your sales, and will be covering more in the pages to come. First, however, it is important to understand the competition and how to make your products more attractive to the potential buyers.

For years, individuals seeking a compact, dependable automobile were buying the Volkswagen Beetle—myself included. After a decade of resistance, manufacturers like Ford and General Motors finally introduced their own line of smaller cars. Almost overnight, VW sales dropped. Why? Because there was now a more attractive product on the market and people always want something new, something different, and something that offers just a little more.

The same can be said about editors. Day in and day out they receive manuscripts. Their guidelines say 1,200 words. They get 1,200 words—over and over and over again. Then, out of the blue, an inspiration falls on their desk. That inspiration should be you.

I like to think of my editorial packages as shiny, new Fords, with metallic paint, while those of others are used, rusted-out VWs. When an editor gets my submission, I can imagine her smile. Why? Because I make her job easy—and so can you. In doing so, you will also rise from the slush pile to the ranks of "most desired" writers.

Because I have worked to create confidence with editors, I am now at a point in my career that I rarely have to provide a query letter for an assignment. Yesterday was a good example. I was offered an opportunity to interview Renzo Rosso, founder and president of Italy's Diesel fashion house. I immediately sent an e-mail to several publications around the world—*Mabuhay* (Philippines), *Italia* (United States), *R&R Magazine* (Germany), *Diplomat* (United Kingdom), *Informer* (Italy), and Articles International (a syndication outfit in Canada). The fact that I have worked with the editors at each of these publications and have become one of their trusted writers, allowed me to write:

> I have just been given an exclusive interview with Renzo Rosso, founder and president of Diesel, Italy's radical, racy, and wildly successful fashion house. With global sales reaching toward the $1 billion mark, Diesel has become the "bad boy" of Italian trends— and the young, active buyers of the world love 'em.
>
> Can I interest you in, say, a 1,500-word feature, a sidebar on the expanding Diesel stores, and another on the company's Internet Web site (where people can order the latest fashions)? As always, I will also provide a vast array of images.

This two-paragraph message gained me three assignments and $1,500.

I'm a firm believer in breaking the rules. In doing so, I've been able to survive—and maintain a family of four—in this cutthroat business of writing for over twenty years. Most books on freelance writing will tell you the standard approach to sell to editors is a formal query letter. While that works, I have experienced ample success with a simple one-line e-mail. Also, during the writing, perhaps I'll find that 2,000 words are needed to do justice to my subject. Despite the editor's request for 1,500 words, I might simply give him 2,000. The key is not to get locked into the traditional mentality of "this is how it's done." Keep an open mind. Be creative. Don't be afraid to experiment. That's how new and better products come about—a car, a mousetrap, an article, or a book.

Here are a few rules, however, that all guerrilla marketers *should* adhere to, if they want to set their products apart from the crowd:

- Always offer to write your first feature on spec. Working with a new editor, on assignment, entails a risk on his part. Who is to say you will come through with what you've promised? To avoid this hesitation, offer your first piece at no obligation. You should have enough confidence in your writing ability and skill in targeting the readership of the publication to believe that the editor will accept the completed story. At the same time you want to stipulate that, in the event that the article is not right, you will be given an opportunity to rewrite. This is how I broke into *Robb Report, Club International,* and *Company* (United Kingdom).
- Always provide more than what's asked for. Let's say you've succeeded in selling a story idea on archaeological expeditions. The editor said 1,000 words should be sufficient. In addition to the article, however, write one or two sidebars of, say, 50

to 150 words each. These might include a list of names and addresses where readers can write for additional information, or perhaps a small interview with an expedition leader. If at all possible, provide photographs and, in this particular case, you might toss in a drawing of an actual archaeological site. These items are frequently available free of charge from the PR departments of the organizations you mention in the article. If you focus on several groups, you might even include the logos of each. These can be used in the layout of the feature. Whatever you do, provide a complete package. This makes the editor's life easier because she does not have to spend time and money searching for illustrations. It also allows the art director greater design freedom because of the array of material you have provided. By offering more, you give the publication the option of using more and, thus, paying you more. The bottom line is that everyone wins and, in the eyes of the client, you become a highly valued writer (a member of the elite).

- Always deliver BEFORE the required deadline. This gives editors more time to review the manuscript and, if needed, make changes or even request rewrites.
- Always offer one free rewrite.
- Include a copy of your article on computer disk. If you provide only a hard copy, the editor must retype the article. Since you have already put in the keystrokes to get the piece into your computer, take the extra time to offer it on disk and in a standard format (Microsoft Word, WordPerfect, etc.).

These are very simple rules to follow, but they will ensure that you and your products are sufficiently different from those that editors normally receive—and will therefore make a lasting impression. Packaging and sales approach are also extremely important in your product marketing; we'll cover those areas in an upcoming chapter. At this point your focus should be on what you are offering—your product—and ways to make it the best.

Better Book Projects

Sooner or later a writer's line of products will normally include books. Here, too, you should not be afraid to take a nontraditional approach—either in your sales pitch or your completed product. Remember: Your goal is to make your work unique and desirable.

The same concepts that applied to your writing service and articles can carry over into book projects. That is, completing your work prior to the deadline, offering more than mere text, indicating a willingness to work with editors on rewrites and changes, and constantly seeking ways in which to expand your line.

Today, the book publishing industry is extremely competitive. One way to avoid competition, however, is to offer a product that only you can produce. In 1985, for instance, Paula Begoun, a makeup artist, wrote *Blue Eye Shadow Should be Illegal* (now published as *The Beauty Bible*). The book was an immense success. She then followed up with *Don't Go to the Cosmetics Counter Without Me*. A few years later, her third book, *Don't Go Shopping for Hair Care Products Without Me*, hit bookstores across the country. Today more than 2 million copies of Begoun's books have been sold.

But the entrepreneur-author did not stop there. She followed the guerrilla marketing technique of expanding her product line. She started a newsletter, *Cosmetics Counter Update*, and now has six thousand subscribers. This venture alone grosses more than $200,000 a year. In 1995, Begoun also began a syndicated beauty column, which is currently run in thirty newspapers, including the *New York Daily News* and the *Houston Chronicle*. Profiting from her name recognition as an author, she put together four romantic travel books and packaged them into the *Best Places to Kiss* series.

The latest venture in Paula Begoun's seemingly never-ending business is a skin care line and new mail-order catalog operation called Sealed with a Kiss.

"Clearly," says Begoun, "[expanding one's product line offers] financial gain. After all, more people see your name and become familiar with your expertise and rely on your information. More important is the ability to get your information out to a wider audience. After all the book-buying population is relatively small compared to the country as a whole."

A sufficient amount of Begoun's time is also spent in marketing herself for lectures and personal appearances. Highlighting herself as an author, a cosmetics expert, and a successful businesswoman has resulted in several appearances on *Oprah,* as well as many other TV and radio talk shows. Each appearance generates more public interest in her work, her products, and her services. As a result, sales of her books, newsletter, and cosmetics soar. In turn, more and more publishers seek her out to produce new works. It's a never-ending cycle of money-making opportunities. And that is what successful guerrilla marketing is all about.

I know. I hear what you're saying. That's fine for her—because she's already successful—but what about *me?*

Anyone can and should play the spin-off game—using one product, one sale, to generate others. It's the momentum theory. Remember our snowball analogy? As it moves downhill it's growing as it picks up more and more snow. At the same time, it moves faster and faster, getting harder to stop. This is what happens when writers use the spin-off approach in their business.

Last year I authored *The Writer's and Photographers Guide to Global Markets* for Allworth Press. Everyone at the company—publisher, editor, promotion, and sales staff—were excited about the book and the excellent reviews it received. On the tailwind of this enthusiasm—and before it cooled—I seized the opportunity to propose a follow-up title that filled a need in the publisher's book line. You are holding the results.

I did not stop there, however. I used the rave reviews from that first book to entice more than six editors to purchase articles on the topic of global marketing for writers and photographers. The snowball was in motion.

Next, an editor asked me to write a monthly "Mike's International Picks" column. Still another—*Writer On Line*—hired me as a contributor to produce a feature titled "Going Global with Mike Sedge." I was then able to use these to spin off an online course for writers called "Going Global with Your Writing Career."

This is just one of many, many examples of marketing spin-offs. In most cases, you will have to work fast to profit from the opportunities your services and products generate. For instance, when *Newsweek* asked me to write a feature on Italian fashions, the magazine insisted on all rights. At $1 a word, I agreed to this with the stipulation that I was free to write new articles for other publications based on my research.

My motives were twofold: (1) *Newsweek* would be paying me for the time I spent researching; and (2) using the *Newsweek* assignment as a springboard, I would gain instant credibility with other publications I approached. And I was correct. Within one week after the original story appeared, I had Italian fashion assignments from *Diplomat* (United Kingdom), *Mabuhay* (Philippines), *Informer* (Italy), and *Silver Kris* (Singapore). I produced two articles—one went to the first three, the other to the last one, because its readership overlapped that of *Mabuhay.*

Over the years I have developed a plus-two formula for business success. Each time I provide a service or product, I try to get at least two spin-off benefits. In the case of the *Newsweek* article, I received four. With my book, *The Writer's and Photographer's Guide to Global Markets,* there were many—and they are still coming in. As a result of this work, I was invited to speak before writers' groups in California, New York, and Washington. Each lecture generated more book sales and more exposure for me. A week after my California appearance, for instance, I received a call from an editor interested in a story on Rome. She said, "I got your name from Jane Sampson, a contributing editor in San Diego. She pointed out that you live in Italy and highly recommended you."

Jane, of course, had met me during my recent lecture.

Your articles can often spin off into books as well. During the onset of the adventure travel boom, I was producing features on hiking in the Alps; bicycling along the Italian coast; exploring the volcanoes of Italy; diving among sunken Roman cities; and even panning for gold a short distance from Milan. Using these as a proposal base, I landed a book contract with publisher Michael Hunter for *The Adventure Guide to Italy.*

Spin-offs and cross marketing are excellent ways in which to sell more of your services and products to potential buyers. Don't try to bite off too much all at once, however. Staying with the plus-two theory, you can increase your sales at a steady, controllable pace. You may have noticed, above, that my book on global marketing ultimately led to organizations seeking my services as a lecturer. Here is where we look at your final "product." That is, you.

In 1988, after a series of marketing efforts to promote myself, I was featured in such publications as *Small Business Opportunities* and *Entrepreneur* (more on how you, too, can get such coverage in the following chapters). This coverage and good networking resulted in a call from MCI Communications. MCI had a need in its marketing department for someone with my skills, not only for hands-on work, but to train others.

"We'd like to contract you for your abilities," said senior manager Randall Slocum.

At that moment, I realized that I was a product. Because of my self-marketing, one of the largest companies in the United States was about to hire me to fill a need—not based on my many published works, nor my knack to write on demand, but because of my *knowledge* and ability to teach it to others. During the next six years I would make over $300,000 from MCI. Why? Because my product (me) filled a need.

You too can fill such needs by examining your own talents. What groups would pay you to lecture? To teach? What can you offer businesses that will help them increase their profits? Remember: The flip side of filling a need is putting yourself in the client's shoes. What is his ultimate goal in hiring you?

In his book *Empire Building by Writing and Speaking*, Gordon Burgett says, "I believe that each of us knows something that others want to know or should know. What you know, or could, is the seed of your empire. And you share that kind of knowledge through writing and speaking."

When marketing yourself as a product, never limit your activities. Had I focused my efforts on, say, local newspapers, *Entrepreneur* would have never featured me and, as a result, the MCI job would have gone to someone else. Likewise, as a writer you should market/promote yourself to a wide range of media outlets—as an author, a lecturer, a teacher, or a talk show guest.

Too often, writers—particularly early in their careers or those living far from a major city—feel they have nothing of value to offer. If you are in this category, you need to study your "product" a little more closely. An increasing number of radio and television talk show producers are turning to writers with a specific area of expertise. Let's say, for instance, that you have recently written a feature on Christmas cookies for *Family Circle.* You completed the story in July because of the lead time required for magazine production. This gives you five months to promote yourself as "This Year's Christmas Cookie Expert." Your subtitle might read, "Learn the tips and tricks of creating unique Holiday Season cookies from (your name), as reported in the December issue of *Family Circle.*"

"I made guest appearances on QVC as an expert on fashions and figure problems to help sell clothes," explained writer, speaker, and consultant Jan Larkey. Ultimately, her book, *Flatter Your Figure,* was released by Simon & Schuster/Fireside in paperback and she was able to arrange a "Fashion Day" with the producers of QVC, selling the title for $10.

"We sold ten thousand copies in that one day!"

"I am writing a book on a work made for hire basis for a book packager. It's a paperback about a popular TV program. I'll be paid $10,000."

—*Meryl Davids, ASJA member*

In today's marketplace, more and more writers are exploring the work offered by book packagers. Like publishers, a packager comes up with an idea for a title, finds the writer, puts together any graphics, and sometimes even handles the layout and design. The difference is that packagers sell their product, prior to production, directly to publishers for a fixed price, plus bonuses.

Many packagers work with television or film tie-ins. I recently worked on such a project and, as with most cases, was offered a flat $1 per word fee for all rights. Considering I was being asked to write 20,000 words, I was more than happy to accept the offer.

Because packagers, in most cases, come up with their own book topics, then seek out writers to do the work, the best approach is to mail a professional press kit (discussed in chapters 7 and 10) and offer your services. For a listing of book packagers check a current edition of *Literary Market Place* or Bookwire on the Internet *www.bookwire.com*.

Thoroughly understanding the services and products you have to offer potential customers will make it easier to create a successful marketing strategy. Considering that your business consists of three sectors—writer for hire (service), articles and books (products), and yourself (product)—you should spend time exploring ways in which to enhance each area, making them more attractive to the customer and, therefore, eliminating the competition. In the day-to-day media battle, you, as a guerrilla marketer, must consider each segment of your business as a task force. Each has the ability to achieve success on its own. Working together, as a team, however, your writing service, your articles, your books, and your personal appearances can blanket the battlefield, cover more territory, and ensure a major victory. You must go into each battle with confidence and a winning spirit. There is no one more qualified than you are to fill your client's needs. There is no other writer who can produce work as well as you. There is no other individual who has the knowledge and ability to pass it on to others as well as you do. This is the mentality required to go into battle. Once you have this, you're ready for the attack.

THE ATTACK

L iving in Europe, I had never heard Rush Limbaugh's radio program, though I was well aware of his controversial fame. Then, during a business trip to Atlanta—and for no particular reason—I picked up Limbaugh's audiotape *The Way Things Ought To Be*. Throughout the two-and-a-half-hour, politically motivated dialogue, Rush made numerous statements, some convincing, some less so. One in particular, however, caused me to instantly admire this man.

He said: "You will never be your best doing it someone else's way. Particularly if you utilize talent as opposed to learned skills. I am convinced that you have absolutely no idea how good you can be at whatever you want to do. You just don't know that because you are trapped into situations where you either can't be yourself or you are afraid to be yourself."

The reason I enjoyed this phrase is because it echoed my own view of life, work, creativity, and, yes, marketing. With regard to marketing, I'd even go one better than Rush by saying that while you can learn from others, you must have the confidence and determination to use what you have learned, to work with that knowledge, and to mold it until it becomes uniquely yours. Nowhere is this more important than in your sales approach.

Individuals who are making a name for themselves in the writing business are those who have such confidence that they cast tradition to the wind and, to quote a seventies cliché, "Do their own thing." While others are following the query-only rule, these name writers are submitting complete editorial packages. When book editors are sending out rejection slips stating, "We only read submissions from agents," this aggressive breed of writers are having lunch with the editors in chief, and selling them on their ideas.

More than anything else, successful guerrilla marketing requires total confidence, a willingness to venture off the beaten path, to experiment with nontraditional sales methods, and, when needed, a willingness to break any and all rules. An excellent illustration of this happened to me just this month.

I'd come up with a nonfiction book idea based on an Italian dog. My marketing research indicated mass sales potential among dog lovers and people interested in true-life, Italian cultural tales—like those found in Frances Mayes's bestseller *Under the Tuscan Sun*. While I worked on the full-blown book proposal, I investigated possible publishers. Near the top of my list was Two Dog Press, a small company known for quality, hardcover titles and a good distribution system—just what the project needed (besides, I really liked the company's logo). While an e-mail address was listed, the guidelines said: "No e-mail submissions."

So I asked myself: Does that mean no query submissions, no proposal submissions, or no complete manuscripts by e-mail? I then decided it meant all three, but what the hell. I zipped off a three-page, e-mail query to editor Karen Kaiser. A week later she replied: "You might be barking up the right tree with this one." (I thought that was cute, too.) She then went on to ask me to send a hard copy of the complete proposal. Nearly a month passed before I received a "not for us" rejection.

Now the rules of tradition say that, at this point, I should have moved on to another publisher. But I kept thinking how nice that Two Dog Press logo would look on a book cover. By the end of the day, my guerrilla instincts had taken control as I sent a follow-up e-mail to Karen asking: "What didn't you like about the book idea?"

This initiative began a chain of communications and ultimately led her to say, "If you want to try and rework one chapter or scene, I'd be willing to take a second look." Needless to say, I leaped at the opportunity and, as I write this, await Kaiser's answer. If you happen to see my name on a book about an Italian dog in the next year—with a great-looking Two Dog Press logo—you'll know I was successful.

The point here is not my success or failure in selling this single project. It is the never-say-die attitude with which I approached the sale. Most writers in my position would have accepted the initial rejection and moved on. I was confident enough, however, to ask why. What was the problem? How could I resolve it? Let me write to "your" needs, rather than mine. Some will disagree with this approach because they are caught up in the creativity of writing rather than the sale. My view on this is that you can be the most creative person in the world, but if your work never reaches the bookstore, or the newsstands, it is not doing you, or others, any good.

Aggressive, nontraditional marketing and a willingness to write to an editor's needs can often be the keys to your success. In today's marketplace, in fact, this approach and attitude are frequently the factors that result not only in increased business, but in better-paying jobs as well.

Perhaps you are sitting in Down-the-Blues, Kentucky, and the only thing you've ever published is a local newspaper article. Who are you to question an editor's authority? Who are you to break the rules? My friend, you are just the same as any other writer. The only difference—as Rush Limbaugh would quickly point out—is that "you just don't know that because you are trapped into situations where you either can't be yourself or you are afraid to be yourself."

Whether you work from a Beverly Hills mansion or a tiny, one-room apartment in SoHo has no bearing on an editor's decision about prospective articles and books. That's one of the better aspects of the writing business: It doesn't discriminate. The fact that editors are not dealing with you face to face—unless you wish to do so—gives you the ability to present your tiny, one-person business as a vast and growing empire. It gives you the opportunity to become the CEO and president of a media agency. It gives you the power to influence the world with your words. In short, as a writer with guerrilla marketing savvy, you can build enough confidence and aggressiveness to establish the rules of the game—and that game is called "Market Attack."

Once you've gathered your intelligence information (that is, figured out client needs) and surveyed your weapons (your services and your products), you're ready for the attack. How are you going to let potential customers know about your writing service? How are you going to sell your articles? Your books? Yourself?

In writing this book, I have been anticipating this chapter. The art of selling, in my opinion, holds a real challenge. It's fun. Exciting. Over the years, selling my work and myself has become a game of strategy and skill. Writing, on the other hand, is hard *work*.

The Agent Myth

A myth hovers over today's publishing industry, one that many writers have been lured into believing. The myth: No book editor will consider your work unless a literary agent represents it. How untrue. In my twenty-year writing career I've had six agents—a couple of them among New York's top ten moneymakers, the others quite a ways down the ladder. Just the same, each provided the same results—nothing. In fact, while they were—as one of them pointed out—"getting my work reviewed by leading editors"—I was busy selling five books and contributing to seven others.

I believe that somewhere—perhaps at the Bronx Zoo on a hot, August afternoon in front of the monkey cage—all of New York's book editors got together and came up with the phrase, "No unsolicited submissions accepted." This is one of the most misleading statements in publishing. Reading it, many novice writers think to themselves, "Oh, shoot. I need an agent."

I am here to tell you that that is *not* what this phrase means at all. Don't read between the lines. Simply read no *unsolicited* submissions. A very important word, unsolicited. It doesn't say *unagented* submissions. An unsolicited work merely indicates one that the editor has not specifically requested. Editors are basically saying to writers, "Hey, we're busy people. We buy particular types of work. Don't be sending your manuscript without first checking to ensure that it is right for us."

I can live with this—have been for many years. And so can you.

Your first step in marketing a book project, therefore, is to get the editor to ask for it. Depending on whether yours is a work of fiction or nonfiction, there are different approaches. For novels, your approach should be in the form of a synopsis. For nonfiction, on the other hand, you can send a simple letter or an overview of the project. Whatever the case, it should be as short as possible while conveying the essence of the book. Don't make the editor work to say yes. If the idea is good and your presentation concise and easy to read, it becomes painless for editors to say, "Sure, send it to me." After all, they are not committing to buying it, but merely to taking a look.

I begin all nonfiction book proposals with an overview of the project. I also use this as my query. This includes the title, author, type of book—fiction, nonfiction—approximate length, and how long it will take to complete the writing. If I am proposing an illustrated work, I also include the number of illustrations, whether color or black and white, and so on. All this information allows the editor to (1) get a feel for the project, (2) calculate the possible cost of producing it, (3) mentally schedule the work into the production calendar, and (4) get a general idea of my writing style (see sample below).

Sample Nonfiction Query

FETTUCCINI FOR THE FRUSTRATED SOUL
(Misadventures of an American in Italy)
by
Michael H. Sedge

TITLE: Fettuccini for the Frustrated Soul
(Misadventures of an American in Italy)

AUTHOR: Michael H. Sedge
TYPE: Nonfiction
LENGTH: 55,000–60,000 Words
COMPLETION DATE: Six months after contract signing.

OVERVIEW

To the delight of Gabriella, his Italian wife, American writer Michael Sedge has set aside this particular Saturday to clean the storage area. It's more than mere cleaning, though. For, hidden away in dark corners, in dusty, taped boxes, and on long, mahogany shelves, this special area holds traces of Sedge's twenty-four years of living and working in southern Italy. Like Pandora's box, object after object unlocks the memories of this stranger in a strange land.

It's a roller-coaster ride of emotions as Sedge tells the stories—often unbelievable, often hilarious, and sometimes serious—of more than two decades of survival in this Mediterranean peninsula.

Like the tales of best-selling author Peter Mayle, the author's experiences will delight readers around the world; whether they are armchair travelers, dreamers, or just out for good entertainment.

Unlike most expat writers, however, Sedge's misadventures seem to have come direct from the script of a box-office hit comedy. Travel along as he ventures to the Abruzzo National Park to fish for brown trout in a clear mountain stream, only to discover—after being caught himself—that it is a government-stocked river.

Imagine the fear when twenty-six antiterrorist *Carabiniere* surround his apartment building and make a raid on his home because they suspect him of planning an attack on the local NATO base.

"When I walked into the street, I thought I'd stepped into the annual Festival of San Antonio," Sedge says. "Lights were flashing, people were screaming, neighbors were hanging like laundry from their balconies to see the 'American terrorist.'"

Live the frustrations and the humor, as he is lined up—despite having lived in the country for twenty years—with illegal immigrants when he tries to renew his sojourner's permit.

Take a trip down memory lane through a five-year court case for an automobile accident. Experience the relief when he ultimately wins his case. Live the frustration when he receives no damages because the other party died three years earlier—as did the first judge. Bottom line: a $1,500 bill from his lawyer.

"Italy must be taken with very large doses of humor," Sedge explains. "How else could you accept making $7 worth of telephone calls, getting a bill for $36, and consider it normal?"

These are just a few of the vignettes, which a summer cleaning reveals from an American in Italy. But where and how did it all begin? And why did Sedge decide to stay?

"I became obsessed with the beauty and love of an Italian girl," he says. "Not to mention the Italian people and their family ties, which have long been lost in much of the world."

So step aboard this fast-moving train of emotions and laughter as it travels to southern Italy. Our first stop is titled: "Help! I'm in Love with an Italian."

In a separate cover letter, I will introduce myself, perhaps mention published works, and ask if I may send the completed proposal for consideration. There are a surprisingly large number of writers who never ask what they want from an editor—assuming, perhaps, that editors have some special telepathic knowledge of what you, the writer, are looking for. Fortunately, for me, I had lunch with such an editor/friend early in my career and asked, "Did you read my letter on Marine Corps Amphibious Assaults?"

"Yes," he replied. "Good idea."

I looked at him, puzzled. "Why didn't you ask me to send the complete proposal?"

"I didn't know that's what you wanted."

From that day on, I always conclude my queries or cover letters with such wording as "May I send the completed proposal for your consideration?" Or, "I welcome the opportunity to provide the completed proposal for your consideration." In the case of fiction, I offer to send the first fifty pages.

Like many guerrilla marketers, I am impatient. I want an answer yesterday. For this reason, I tend to go against the grain and e-mail my queries to editors. I also like to machine-gun submissions. That is, produce one e-mail query and send it to as many as fifty editors simultaneously. If you must make a living putting words on paper, time is a very important aspect of your business. You cannot wait years to sell your book ideas. Had McDonald's sold door to door, the company never would have reached the billion-burger mark—and neither will you.

In utilizing e-mail queries, of course, writers run the risk of never receiving a reply, for a number of reasons. Some editors simply do not accept e-mail queries. Others have their e-mail screened by assistants, and your idea may never reach them. More often than not, however, if an editor is not keen about your idea, she will merely delete your message, because it is so easy to do so. With the click of a mouse, it is as if your query never existed.

Personally, I'm willing to take the risk involved in e-mail queries. In my view, editors who see sales potential in your idea will reply. If I do not hear from an editor within a week, I merely assume he is not interested and move on. I've saved myself time and money. The publishing pond is big. You simply reel in your line at this point and cast into another part of the lake. There, perhaps, a bigger fish will bite instantly. Whether large or small, the key is that you are catching fish.

Three weeks ago, for instance, Ted Salois, a long-time friend and two-time Military Photographer of the Year, sent me a proposal on the U.S. Navy's Special Forces (SEAL) units asking if I could help sell it. In my view, the concept was excellent. I, in turn, sent the following e-mail to several editors.

To: Jeff Smith / ABC Books
From: Michael Sedge / Strawberry Media

Dear Jeff,
Award-winning U.S. military photojournalist Ted Salois retired from the U.S. Navy recently and has put together one of the finest nonfiction, illustrated book proposals I have ever seen. The topic: NAVY SEALS: The Sharpest Blade.

As the author points out: "Navy SEALs are known and respected around the globe for their superb abilities, courage, endurance, and rate of success—no SEAL has ever been captured by an enemy force and no SEAL fatality has ever been left behind."

In the proposal's "Approach" section, Salois says: "Approximately 35,000 lively words and 200 beautifully detailed color photographs will guide the reader through each and every page of 'NAVY SEALs: The Sharpest Blade' as it tells of the SEALs' history and relates the grit and determination that SEAL candidates possess and bring to bear to their physical and technical training to become one of the best of the United States' elite special forces."

I welcome the opportunity to provide you with a copy of the proposal for consideration as an ABC Books title, if you are interested.

Looking forward to your reply.

Sincerely,

Michael Sedge
Via Venezia 14/b

80021 Afragola (NA) Italy
Tel: (011) 39-081-851-2208
Fax. (011) 39-081-851-2210

Within two hours, Tom Dunne (Thomas Dunne Books/St. Martin's Press) and Jonathan Karp (Random House) both requested that I send them the complete proposal.

That's the way I like to do business.

The e-mail addresses of book editors are not readily available in most cases. Why? Editors do not want to be swamped by thousands of electronic submissions. If you can find the general e-mail format of a publishing company, however, you can often come up with the addresses of specific editors on your own. For example, Random House and its subsidiaries utilize, for the most part, the first initial, the last name, and @randomhouse.com. So, if you were sending an e-mail to Mary Doe, it would be *mdoe@randomhouse.com*. Similarly, if you have a project that you feel is perfect for the Discovery Channel, you'd find their e-mail format is in the format of firstname_lastname@discovery.com. So Mary Doe would receive electronic mail at *Mary_Doe@discovery.com*.

Last week I had a proposal that, I felt, was perfect for Simon & Schuster's (S&S) trade paperback division. Rather than utilizing information in reference books that might very well have been outdated, I found senior editor Becky Cabaza's name in a current edition of *Publisher's Weekly*. It did not, however, provide an e-mail address.

I next began to search the Internet for S&S links— there were several. Most of them provided an e-mail for ordering or obtaining information. I noted that the S&S Consumer Group's e-mail addresses fell under Prentice Hall. For example, *sales@prenhall.com* or *info@prenhall.com*. Then it was merely a matter of experimentation. First, I sent my query to *bcabaza@prenhall.com*. Within seconds it came back with "unknown address." I then tried *becky_cabaza@pren-hall.com.* Success!

Ms. Cabaza ultimately turned down my idea, but the time and money saved by the e-mail query made the rejection much easier to take.

I'd like to share one more example of e-mail book queries with you because it illustrates my point so perfectly and because it came in less than twenty minutes ago. This time I sent Mort Castle, publisher at Thorby Enterprises, a synopsis for *PAURA!* a horror novel that has won a number of awards but is still unpublished. I transmitted the e-mail query three days ago, to which Castle replied: "You know, this is literate; that's the only reason I read it . . . a brief synopsis means nothing to me. Anyone can write a synopsis . . . which is one of the reasons I state, in our fairly detailed guidelines, that this sort of query is just what I don't want to see. Now, given all this, your being literate has still managed to keep your proverbial ship afloat. I'd like to have our science-fiction/fantasy guy give a first reading to the first thirty pages of this; that should be accompanied by a detailed, chapter by chapter outline of the rest of the book, as well as the standard SASE."

He was, obviously, not pleased to receive the e-mail query. Yes, he was upset about the format and the fact that I had gone against the publishing house's guidelines. But he was interested in the work, its merit, and its potential for sales. Thus, my theory proved true once again. If an editor likes the project, he will ask to see more.

The guerrilla marketer wins one more battle by using quality and strategy, rather than textbook tactics.

Once an editor has asked you to submit your work, it is no longer "unsolicited." Because book editors, in most cases, do not open their own mail, be sure to include a cover letter reminding them that the material was requested. This will automatically alert the secretary or editorial assistant to place your submission in the "to read" pile rather than the trash or slush pile.

Okay, I know some of you—mostly veterans—are saying to yourself, "This guy is out of touch. I receive rejections all the time that specifically say, 'No unagented submissions!'"

What can I say? You are right. There are a growing number of editors adopting this policy; particularly in this day and age, when readers and associate editors are becoming extinct due to editorial budget reductions. The industry has learned that good literary agents can take the place of midlevel publishing personnel at no cost to the publishers. So why shouldn't it use agents as unpaid staff? It's simply good business.

In these cases, however, what do you—an unagented author—do to get your projects into the hands of, and read by, acquisitions editors? Very simply, lace up your combat boots because you're going to become a guerrilla literary agent.

The Self Agent

Earlier I stressed that you should operate as a business, preferably under a name different than your own. One of the primary reasons for this is that it allows you certain freedoms. For example, the freedom to represent yourself as a literary agent. Certainly, there are those who will argue that I am walking a fine line here, that most writers do not have the experience, the credentials, or the contacts to be a "reputable" agent. That, in my view, is absurd.

Even though I have had numerous agents, I have also been representing myself for years—and very successfully, I might add. All my work as an agent has been conducted with the utmost professionalism, with personal contacts—or through networking, whereby I was introduced by other editors or agents—and by maintaining high-quality, salable products. After all, that, and only that, is what the editors and publishers are interested in. If I were an agent in, say, South Africa and offered the latest Wilbur Smith work to the editors of Bantam, Putnam, St. Martin's Press, or Simon & Schuster, I seriously doubt that any of them would know me. At the same time, I'm fairly certain they would all be interested in what I offered. Why? Because Smith's books sell. And that is the pure reality of today's publishing industry: It must sell and sell well.

I got into self-agenting years ago, when an associate editor sent me one of those irritating, preprinted rejection slips: "We only accept submissions through agents." My marketing mind suddenly went into overdrive as I thought, perhaps it's time my "media business" expanded to include literary services and representation. But whose name would sign the correspondence, as I was the author, editor, manager, and owner of this one-man operation? Then, like an angel, the answer walked through the door.

My wife, Gabriella, loves to spend money, so what better person to be my literary representative than she? After all, if she is going to spend it, why not help make it? Another reason to utilize my wife's name was to ensure that any mail or inquiries were addressed to a person who actually existed. Oh, yes, there is also another reason, so smoothly pointed out by Gabriella. If a contract is awarded, you'll need to have a person to sign the contract and cash the checks. (I didn't tell her that I can easily have them made out to Strawberry Media. Why spoil her fun?)

The following day, I prepared a letter on Strawberry Media stationery to a senior editor at the same publishing company that had rejected my nonagented work the previous week. The query read (names changed to protect my future business):

To: Jane Doe / ABC Publishing
From: Gabriella Giugliano / Strawberry Media
Subject: Rudy: Angel on Four Legs

Dear Ms. Doe,
We would like to offer you the opportunity to consid-
er the latest nonfiction project by author Michael
Sedge, *Rudy: Angel on Four Legs*. It is a heartwarming
story of two stray dogs in the southern Italian town of
Afragola, north of Naples.

   Unlike many nonfiction dog titles, *Rudy* does not
provide guidelines for pet owners, or training of any
type. It is, one might say, the canine equivalent of
Bridges of Madison County. It is *Lady and the Tramp* in
reverse. It's *Love Story* between two dogs: Rudy, who
left the comfort and safety of his home to live in the
streets with Lady. More than this, however, it is a
touching tale of a dog's effect on the life of the author
and the tiny Italian community in which they live.

   One might compare Michael Sedge's style with
that of James Thurber, as he invites readers to his
world—and that of Rudy—in the tiny Italian village.

   I welcome the opportunity to provide a copy of the
complete proposal for your consideration, and look
forward to hearing from you.

Sincerely,

Gabriella Giugliano
STRAWBERRY MEDIA AGENCY
Via Venezia 14/b
80021 Afragola (NA) Italy
Tel: (011) 39-081-851-2208
Fax: (011) 39-081-851-2210
E-mail: *pp10013@cybernet.it*

To save time—and to avoid having the query routed to the
associate editor—I faxed the letter. That same afternoon, the
senior editor replied, by fax:

Dear Gabriella,
Mr. Sedge's story sounds intriguing. Please send me
the full proposal at your convenience.

Sincerely,

Jane Doe
Senior Editor
ABC Publishing

Whether the book sold to this editor or not, I felt a sense of
pure satisfaction. I—a freelance writer—had succeeded in
beating the system and getting around the "agented work
only" hurdle. But would it work again? There was only one
way to find out.

Still seeking a publisher for my *Fettuccini for the Frustrated Soul* project, I researched until I came up with individual
editors, and their fax numbers, at five major publishing houses: Ballantine, Alfred A. Knopf, Penguin Putnam, Random
House, and Scribner. Each editor received a query from "Gabriella Giugliano" at the Strawberry Media Agency in Europe.
Over the next week, the following replies were received:

"Thank you for your fax. Mr. Segal will be happy to
consider the proposal."—Ida Giragossian, Assistant to
Jonathan Segal, Alfred A. Knopf

"I am writing on behalf of Kathryn Court in response
to your fax regarding Michael Sedge's *Fettuccini for the
Frustrated Soul*. Ms. Court is indeed interested in seeing
a detailed proposal and would appreciate it if you
could send her one straightaway."—Allen MacDuffie,
Assistant to Kathryn Court, Penguin Putnam, Inc.

"I'd be happy to read the proposal. Go ahead and send
it. Thanks." —Jon Karp, Senior Editor, Trade, Random
House

"Thank you for your fax regarding Michael Sedge's *Fettuccini for the Frustrated Soul*. Scott Moyers is no longer with Scribner, but I would love to take a look at the completed proposal for this book."—Marah Stets, Associated Editor, Scribner

"I am writing on behalf of Maureen O'Neal. If you would like to send Ms. O'Neal sample chapters, she would be happy to review the material. She would need at least a partial manuscript before making any kind of decision."—Steven Gutierrez, Ballantine Publishing

I still utilize agents for particular projects. Last week, for example, I sent a nonfiction, spiritual book proposal to one of the representatives I regularly work with. Why? Because he specializes in this type of work. He can easily call two or three editors in this field, pitch them the idea over the phone, or over a Big Mac, and get a "Send me the full proposal" in response. It might take me weeks or months to obtain a similar answer.

Yesterday, I received an e-mail from this agent stating, "I'll read this over during the weekend and let you know my thoughts. When I opened the package I glanced through the pages out of curiosity. Your use of graphics is impressive."

I told this to a colleague the following day. She reacted with shock. "At a seminar just last week I was told that book proposals were to be straightforward, no gimmicks, no graphics, nothing but the text—and that, too, should be in a sans serif font. Now you are telling me that you sent a cover design, inserted graphics throughout the proposal text, and even used several varieties of fonts? And your agent said that it was impressive?"

My answer—with a smile—was, "Exactly."

I am not the only one who has found success in utilizing graphics, charts, and sidebars in book proposals. Lee

Silber, author of *Career Management for the Creative Person,* sold this work—and other book ideas—with a bound, thirty-two–page proposal that included a color image of the author on the cover, sidebars, over twenty boxed quotes, and a variety of bold headlines and subtitles.

"Lee is very strong in marketing," explained agent Toni Lopopolo. "His book proposals leap out and invite editors to read them. The proposal for *Career Management for the Creative Person* is one of the best I have ever seen."

Coming from a woman who was a top editor for St. Martin's Press for many years, this is a great compliment. But what does it tell you?

Well, here is what it tells me. First, while traditional nonfiction book proposals work, one should not fear experimentation. Second, editors are so deluged with words that they often welcome the opportunity to review well-designed proposals with graphics, sidebars, or any layout that breaks up the monotony of pure text.

Guerrilla marketing, in many ways, is about going against the grain—doing things differently while still maintaining integrity and professionalism. For years corporate executives have successfully sold business plans, for millions of dollars, based on highly visual, well-thought-out, fact-filled presentations. So why can't you sell books the same way? This is particularly true in today's publishing environment, where the bottom line (profit) is more important than the literary value of most work. (If this offends you, I apologize. It is, however, a reality of the contemporary book industry.)

My book proposals normally total forty pages, half of which is dedicated to the marketing aspects of the work. They cover statistics regarding potential buying markets, competing titles and their success, promotional methods to sell the book, and various media to reach primary and secondary markets. This is extremely valuable information for any editor, particularly at large publishing houses. In effect, the editor must become your in-house agent and make a sales pitch to the other departments—sales, production, and so on—at the company. Including as much positive marketing data as possible will only help an editor "sell" your proposal. This is one more way in which you can set your product apart from the rest.

For my spiritual book, *Where Goodness Lies,* for example, the following pages were included to cover the current marketplace. It is, basically, a sales pitch to the editor and his colleagues. To some editors—those who are attuned to the market in which their books sell—the information may not be new. In that case, my facts merely reinforce their knowledge. For others, this may well be the ammunition required to fight the internal battle many editors must go through before they are able to offer you a contract.

Where Goodness Lies by Michael Sedge: Proposal

THE MARKET

The religious, spiritual, and inspirational markets are among the most lucrative in contemporary publishing. Inasmuch as *Where Goodness Lies* carries a distinctly religious theme—Getting to Heaven—its nonpreaching style extends this title into the spiritual and inspirational marketplace, like such best-selling works as *Chicken Soup for the Soul* and *The Road Less Traveled.*

But just how large is this market? One of the best ways to judge the trends of religious and spiritual buyers, according to the Christian Booksellers Association (CBA), is to use the "Bible factor." Simply put, take the number of Bibles sold each year in the United States and you have a fairly good estimate of the number of potential readers for a project like *Where Goodness Lies.*

Britt Beemer of America's Research Group found that Bible sales were up 30–40 percent in the late nineties, with an estimated 168,000 Bibles purchased *daily*.

Ninety-one percent of all households own at least one Bible, and most also have other Christian books.

Barna Research Group Publishers

At the same time, however, today's readers want precise, condensed information that not only inspires them, but is easy to read and comprehend. Too many individuals, when reading spiritual works, ask, "What does this mean for me?" said John Sawyer, marketing director for Zondervan Publishing House. As a result, most people need a "user-friendly interface" between themselves and the complex teachings found in the Bible.

For this reason *Where Goodness Lies,* with its easy-to-understand, day-by-day lessons and message, makes perfect sense for the contemporary marketplace.

At the 1998 CBA International Convention, the buzzword in marketing trends was "category development" or, for veteran booksellers, "segment marketing." Banners telling participants to "Think Kids First!" waved from the exhibition hall. True pros, however, were already thinking that and more.

Forty-five percent of American adults said their spirituality is more important today than three years ago.

—*Survey by Tyndale House Publishers*

"When looking for a bestseller like *Conversations with God,*" said one attendee, "publishers had better think not only kids, but young adults, middle-aged adults, and the elderly."

The concept of *Where Goodness Lies* makes it a potential seller in each of these market segments. Its theme opens the doors for Christian as well as traditional bookstore distribution. Specialty shops, gift stores, and religious outlets like the more than 270 Family Christian Stores are all retail candidates for this unique title. Direct sales to churches and church groups are also possible.

The Internet, too, opens new areas and methods of reaching the vast market for this title. From Amazon.com to FirstNetChristian, (launched on July 15, 1998 by Riverside Distributors for online purchases), this book provides a vast array of marketing opportunities for any sales department.

Selling and marketing of *Where Goodness Lies* will also be aided by CBA's global plan known as "Impact × 2." The goal of this strategy is to double the awareness of Christ by doubling the sales of CBA members' titles over a five-year period. To achieve this, a great deal of effort and marketing money are being put into heightening public awareness of spiritual books. Thus, works like *Where Goodness Lies* can take advantage of this movement and ride the waves into the homes of readers across the nation and the world.

The religious, spiritual, and inspirational markets today support more than 300 major magazines in the United States, according to *Writer's Digest*. The trend in this field is toward a human-interest tone. Something that can be read "at human level."

What is more "human level" than helping others, reaching out to neighbors, friends, and strangers in need? This, after all, is the message of love that God has given to humankind—and one of the keys to Heaven's gate.

By utilizing boxed quotes, I've provided not only a graphic element to break up the text, but answered the question "Who says so?" In other words, it is not Michael Sedge saying that 91 percent of all U.S. households have at least one Bible, but the Barna Research Group. I, therefore, establish credibility as well as my ability to research.

If you recall, I said that filling a need is 70 percent of selling a book. Your influence over an editor's decision lies, primarily, within the remaining 30 percent. To increase the possibilities of selling your product, always consider the following:

- Does your idea have mass market appeal? The larger the potential market, the greater your possibilities of a sale.
- Is the topic something that no one else can write? As the old saying goes, There are no new ideas, simply new approaches. What makes you the perfect writer for this job?
- What role will you play in the marketing of your book? Are you willing to take four-week author tours? Appear on national television? Do radio talk shows? Do you have media contacts that can be used to promote the book?
- Does the idea fill a market segment that current titles do not? Let's say you are going to write a diet book. What makes it unique, different from the thousands of similar titles already on the market?

"When conceiving and writing your books, you too should ask yourself the question, 'Who will buy my book, and why?'" says publisher and author John Kremer, in *1001 Ways to Market Your Books*. "And you had better have a good answer."

Selling a book is much like winning the lottery. It is about having the right idea in the right place at the right time. Have you ever noticed that as soon as a disaster takes place there seems to instantly be a book on the market covering it? How many books on the *Titanic* appeared after the award-winning film hit the theaters? And let's not forget the mother of overnight bestsellers, the White House's response to *Beautiful,* the Sexgate transcripts of Kenneth Starr.

Each of these filled an immediate editorial need. The public was hungry for more information and publishers felt it their duty (to their shareholders, in most cases) to feed that sector of the population.

True guerrilla writers will find inside tracks into trends, and profit from them. They will, additionally, utilize nontraditional formats and design to get quick attention to their proposals. Those who do not posses graphic skills can simply review magazine layouts, find something attractive, and copy that format. This will set their work apart from the crowd—and that is what you are after. At the same time, however, there is no substitute for quality, well-researched text. While the presentation can open the door, it will be your writing abilities that ultimately sell your book.

List Proposals

Literary agent Becky Hardy, in an effort to expose the projects of several clients to a wide market of book editors, produced a brochure containing one-paragraph blurbs on each writer's work, then mass-mailed it to editors around the country. The marketing technique proved fairly successful, and several requests for complete proposals were received. Naturally, after hearing this, I too had to try it.

Like most long-time writers, I constantly have five or six book proposals looking for a home. I, therefore, prepared a letter—from the Strawberry Media Agency—introducing author Michael Sedge and providing two pages of "Current offerings by Michael Sedge." Because I was not printing a brochure, I was able to expand listings to provide a better overview of each project. For example:

MAN & MYTH

THE PHLEGRAEAN FIELDS

The Phlegraean Fields. It was here, in the eighth century B.C., that ancient Greeks first stepped upon what would someday be southern Italy. Here, among volcanic lakes and bubbling waters, myths and legends grew. Homer's Ulysses encountered the Cumaean Sibyl here, and Virgil found Lake Averno the perfect place for his entrance to the underworld.

Today, traces of the underworld, the cave of the Sibyl, as well as an array of Greek and Roman ruins highlight the Phlegraean Fields, one of Italy's relatively unknown archaeological zones.

The sunken city of ancient Baiae rests here, in fifteen to thirty feet of water—including the elegant villa of Roman emperor Claudio. Finds from this submerged city are displayed in the nearby fifteenth-century castle of Baiae, while nearby patrons still use the Stufa di Nerone (Nero's spa), with saunas dug into caves, where natural mineral springs continue to spew steaming waters from the depths of the earth into open baths encompassed by vaulted arches, just as they did in Roman times.

This is the home of ancient Pozzuoli, and the third-largest amphitheater in the world. Here, too, volcanic pools and steam spouts continue to spurt, hiss, bubble, and inspire awe among visitors.

The Phlegraean Fields is where man and myth have merged to create one of the most unique settings of our world. While boasting far more history, mythology, and natural wonder than the surrounding attractions of Pompeii and Mount Vesuvius, very little has been written, or published, about this unique zone of southern Italy, located west of Naples.

Now, author Michael Sedge proposes an illustrated guide to the history, legends, ruins, and natural wonders of The Phlegraean Fields, home of MAN & MYTH.

In all, four projects were included in my "list proposal" package. It was then sent to twenty editors. Within a month, sixteen replies had been received. Eleven said thanks, but no thanks. The remaining five asked for one or more proposals to be sent for their consideration.

Just one more marketing trick for the writer's manual of tactical warfare.

GUERRILLA ARTICLES

_S_ ometimes I feel that writers intentionally make an effort to fail as business people. Take, for example, the thousands of freelancers around the world who write articles. They produce a feature, sell it, see it in print, and then begin work on another story. It too gets written, sold, and printed. Then a new article is begun. It becomes a vicious circle.

Now some would say that this is a pattern of success. I am here to tell you that it is a blueprint for excess work, below-average income, and, ultimately, writer burnout. Why? First, given that the average article of one thousand words sells for approximately $375 in the United States, writers need to produce and sell eight articles a month if they want to earn an annual income of $35,000. Writing this many quality articles every thirty days is a huge task. Then, of course, because freelance writers are independently employed, they are required to spend a large percentage of their annual income on social security taxes, health insurance, and income taxes. After all these taxes and insurance payments are made, most writers—even those selling articles regularly—find themselves walking the tightrope of poverty.

If they would only approach writing as a business, however, this dire situation could probably be avoided. Let's imagine for a moment that you are not a writer, but the franchise owner of Dollar Rent A Car. What are your products? Cars and vans, of course. Now what are your goals? To rent as many vehicles as you can, for as much as you can, and for as long as you can.

Now let's apply these same business characteristics to writing. What are your products? Articles. What are your goals? To sell as many as you can, for as much as you can, and for as long as you can.

Yes, articles, as I pointed out in previous chapters, are products. To succeed, you need to make as much money as possible from these products. The more use—in the form of sales—you get out of each product, the more money you will make. This requires that you set your own rates, control the rights that are sold, and expand your market opportunities beyond domestic borders.

As a businessman, my goal has always been to make no less than $4,000 a month—damned good pay for an article writer. To accomplish this, I am required to bring in $1,000 a week. This leads me to the $1-a-word rule (yes, I have rules for just about everything). Quite simply, if a publication is going to pay me $1 a word, that publication is entitled to exclusive rights to my work for a period of one year. Thereafter, all rights automatically revert to me, and I am free to sell the article elsewhere. As with every rule, however, there are exceptions. If, for instance, a publisher wants a work-for-hire arrangement—whereby the publication owns the work forever—my base fee ranges from $1.50 to $2.00 a word.

So what about the many, many magazines and newspapers that do not have budgets sufficient to pay such rates? Very simply, the rights that a publication receives should be directly proportional to the price paid. I'll even go one step further and say that the rights purchased must *never* exceed the *needs* of the publication. An excellent example is the Army Times Publishing Company, based in Virginia. The company's primary market is Department of Defense employees and members of the U.S. military. So, when travel editor Cindi Florit offered me $225 for a feature on Italy's sunken city of Baiae, I gladly accepted. When she asked for all rights, I pulled back the offer and said Army Times could have exclusive rights only in the Department of Defense and U.S. military market, to which she agreed.

The point here is that many editors, it seems, have been trained—primarily because they too began as freelance writers—to believe that all rights or first North American serial rights are theirs for the asking, as long as they have offered some pittance of compensation. I, for one, would like to know where this absurd thought came from. Army Times Publishing Company had no more need for all rights than does the *Prague Post* in the Czech Republic.

This morning, a reader of my *Writer On Line* column, "Going Global with Mike Sedge," sent a message in which she said: "You suggest that authors establish their own rights, rather than wait and see what an editor offers. It's a concept I've never heard of but find quite compelling and it makes ever so much sense."

Of course it makes sense. It makes good *business* sense! A major part of guerrilla marketing is not to let the excitement of getting published blur your business vision.

That is, you must be fairly compensated for your work and the rights you are selling. The key to rights is that you give each publication what it *needs,* within the legal boundaries of the sale. For example, if a newspaper published in New York State is going to publish your article, it has no *need* for all North American rights. In this same respect, a national publication has no *need* for world rights. If I am working with a periodical that insists on more rights than are necessary, I immediately up the price of the article accordingly.

Recently, *Scientific American Archaeology* asked me to write a piece, but insisted on all rights. I realized that they had plans for an international as well as German-language edition of the magazine and, thus, planned to reuse my material. I therefore quoted a price of $1.25 per word, with the agreement that they would take at least two more features. They agreed to the deal. In this case I had sacrificed some of my standard per-word fee—for all rights usage—in exchange for additional assignments.

Granted, you might lose a sale by doing this. But, in the long run, you will end up making more money by being able to sell your articles again and again. Despite what editors and individuals involved with the New York publishing industry tell you, there are publishers that aggressively resell articles once they have all rights. *Buzz* magazine goes so far as to advertise the resale of articles. A recent issue, for example, carried an ad reading, among other things, "Reprints of any article are now available from Reprints Management Services. Call today."

The War of Rights

While there are certain established rights (for example, first North American serial rights, second serial rights, and reprint rights) there are no rules that say you cannot make up your own rights. I do this all the time, based on a publication's readership. I do a great deal of work for *Going Places Doing Things,* a bimonthly, English-language magazine published in Rome. I offer the publisher first English-language serial rights in Italy, which leaves me free to sell the same articles to an Italian-language publication. If that same article is sold to *Gente Viaggi,* also in Italy, what that publication is buying is first Italian-language serial rights. Similarly, *R&R Magazine,* in Germany, might purchase "exclusive rights in the military market," leaving me free to sell exclusive German-language rights.

You, and not the editor or publisher, should establish what rights are for sale. This is the only way to truly control what you own. I normally do not discuss rights when proposing an article. Some editors, but not most, will offer a written contract once they agree to assign you the story. These agreements spell out the rights that the magazine desires. If you do not agree with them, simply inform the editor of the rights you are offering, change the contract, initial the change, and submit it. This is a common practice and most editors, if you give them the rights they *need,* will agree—though they may have to clear it with the publisher or legal department.

As previously said, I also make up rights. Let's say a newspaper in Genessee County, Michigan, wants an article. I'd offer them one-time rights in Genessee County only. I could then legally sell to the *Detroit Free Press* (different county) and an array of other Michigan papers.

To give you a better idea of some common and not-so-common rights you can offer publications, here is the listing I use (and frequently add to):

- *All Rights* (Frequently referred to as "work for hire")
  If you are writing under this agreement, forget all

hopes of international marketing. The buyer, once you have turned over the article, owns it lock, stock, and barrel.

- *First North American Serial Rights*
These rights are commonly purchased by the first publication, on a national level, that uses your article in North America.

- *Second North American Serial Rights*
Smaller magazines, even regional ones, will often pay a lower price for quality articles, knowing that they have appeared elsewhere. In this case, they are the second publication to use the article in North America. To reconfirm that you are selling only single-usage rights, you can also add "one-time use" to the rights line of these and any other nonexclusive offerings.

- *Reprint Rights*
Newspapers frequently use reprinted material as long as the articles have not appeared in a competing publication. The price is often much lower than you might get for first or second serial rights.

- *Regional Rights*
There will be times when you may want to restrict the sale of rights to a particular city, county, region, or province. This would allow you to sell "first regional rights" throughout a country.

- *Exclusive Language Rights*
Some articles cross the lines of culture, language, and nations. For these, you should consider selling exclusive language rights (such as Spanish, German, Dutch, Italian, and English) when marketing internationally.

- *Exclusive Geographical Rights*
Countrywide rights can also be negotiated for multiple-nation sales.

- *Language and Geographical Rights*
This is one of my favorites, as it limits not only the language but also the geographical area. For instance, if you sell exclusive Spanish-language rights to a publication in Mexico, you cannot sell the same article in Spain. By adding geographical restrictions, however, you are free to sell the same article in numerous countries that speak the same language—for example, exclusive Spanish-language rights in Mexico, Puerto Rico, Spain, and Portugal.

- *Exclusive Market Rights*
Throughout the world there are publishers that are only concerned that an article they run has not and will not appear in a competing magazine or newspaper. In these cases, offer exclusive market rights. In-flight publications are excellent examples. The publishers of these slick, color magazines all want exclusivity in the marketplace.

   You should also be careful to ensure that the type of usage you are offering is completely spelled out. That is, you should make it clear whether you are selling serial rights (for use in periodicals such as newspapers and magazines), book rights, audio rights, motion picture rights, video rights, or what have you. In your case, you will most often be dealing with serial rights. So, if you are selling an article in London, you may be offering first U.K. serial rights. On the other hand, if the story is appearing in a Japanese publication, you may be selling first Japan serial rights or exclusive Japanese-language rights. The latter set of rights would leave you open to also sell exclusive English-language rights in Japan.

- *Electronic Rights*

  In this age of the Internet, electronic rights must be aggressively protected. Many publishers will purchase an article from you under the "assumption" that they can utilize it in both print and electronic media. If they wish to do so, you should negotiate an additional fee for electronic publication over and above the print rights.

  Unlike geographical rights, which can sell over and over, electronic rights, for the most part, are one-time sales. An editor receives your piece and places it in an Internet magazine for anyone in the world to read. The only leverage you may have is to limit the "language" rights. For instance, you can offer exclusive electronic rights in the English language. This leaves you open to sell to Internet magazines in, say, French, Japanese, or German.

  Handling the rights of your product in creative ways is merely one step in operating a successful editorial business. Now you must make those products work for you in the form of sales and re-sales around the world. You must go global with your marketing. There are several ways to illustrate what I mean. One of the best examples, however, is to look at the "Life of a Guerrilla Article," which follows.

  First, though, a couple more rules. If someone offers you $1,000 for an article, take it. If someone offers you $50, take that too. The important factor, as I have said again and again, is that the rights match the cash. Pay less, get less. Pay more, get more. Second, to be a successful business person, you must minimize your work while maximizing your profits. Those who do not live by these two simple rules are merely poor managers of both time and money.

Life of a Guerrilla Article

All articles begin with an idea. While I agree with editors who say narrow the focus of your subject to make it more salable, I also believe that you should keep a broad readership in mind. By doing so, you automatically open the door to multiple sales. Take, for example, archaeology. Several years ago I wrote a feature on the ancient Roman city of Baiae, which, today, lies off the southern Italian coast in ten to thirty feet of water. I could have easily written the tale of a scuba diver and sold it to *Diver Magazine*. Instead, I took a broad approach, focusing on the city's history, famous residents such as Emperor Nero, the contributing causes of the town's destruction, archaeological research and finds, and, ultimately, how contemporary sports divers enjoy exploring the sunken ruins, just as other tourists roam the nearby excavations of Pompeii.

This approach suddenly expands the market from divers to archaeologists, historians, and even armchair travelers. I expanded the potential readership even further during the writing by producing an adventure-style piece—but I'm getting ahead of myself.

As a guerrilla writer, you need to come up with a tasty query—one an editor finds hard to resist. In the case of Baiae, I opened as if I were on an actual dive, effortlessly gliding downward through the haunting, blue-green Mediterranean waters with eerie ruins coming into view. Upon completion of my query, I loaded my IBM and began a series of "machine gun" submissions.

Arky Gonzalez, a well-known journalist and active member of the American Society of Journalists and Authors, is famous for his mass-submission techniques. So is Austria-based writer Nino LoBello, whose byline appears in perhaps one hundred publications around the world each year, though not necessarily on one hundred different articles. Like myself, Arky and Nino have discovered that, with a good query and business savvy, they can sell the same article ten, twenty, or even a hundred times.

Initially, the query on the underwater city of Baiae went out to twenty publications from Asia to Africa and Australia to Europe. Where possible, the proposal was sent by e-mail. In other cases, it was transmitted by fax. Four submissions—to editors for whom I had no fax number and who despised electronic submissions—were sent via snail mail. Within a week I received an acceptance: *Oceans* took first North American serial rights.

While the other queries continued to circulate, I began work on the article. Knowing that I would be selling the story to global markets, I decided to avoid American slang, phrases, comparisons, and expert quotes. I chose to utilize metric measures rather than feet and inches because the latter are utilized almost exclusively in the United States (there may be one other nation in the world). Finally, I chose an adventure theme to ensure that my goal of multiple, worldwide sales would be achieved. After all, action-adventure films like *Indiana Jones, Stargate,* and even *Six Days, Seven Nights* all earned enormous international success.

Prior to sending out the queries, I had created a "Sales/Marketing" chart—something I suggest to all aggressive writers. More than a mere listing of where your submissions go, the Sales/Marketing chart is a companion to the marketing research you do to target potential buyers of your product—in this case, your article. The first step in producing a chart is to decide in which geographic areas you will focus your sales efforts. In my case, I chose Australia, Bahrain, Germany, Hong Kong, Italy, Kuwait, the Philippines, Scandinavia, South Africa, the United Kingdom, and the United States. In making these choices, I asked the following questions: (1) What publications am I aware of in these countries that are potential buyers? (2) What rights can I offer each publication without overlapping circulation or running into conflicts? (3) What is the best approach— e-mail, fax, letter.

Armed with this information, I compiled my Sales/Marketing chart. Under each country, I listed the potential markets, the rights I would offer, the method and date of query. For example:

BAHRAIN
- *Golden Falcon*
  Exclusive in-flight magazine rights in English/Arabic
  E-mail—August 29

GERMANY
- *GEO*
  Exclusive German-language serial rights
  Fax—August 29

- *Leisure Time*
  Exclusive Canadian military market rights in Europe
  Fax—August 29

- *Overseas*
  Exclusive U.S. military market rights in Europe
  Fax—August 29

ITALY
- *Going Places Doing Things*
  English-language rights in Italy only
  Fax—August 29

- *SUB*
  Italian-language rights in Italy only
  E-mail—August 29

By the time the article was written—and I had added a selection of images and maps to the completed package—I had sold exclusive U.S. military market rights to *Overseas* in Germany. Whenever a rejection letter came in, I simply sought another publication within the geographic area to which I could offer the same rights I had proposed to the first publication. To each one of those that ultimately accepted my offer, I submitted the completed package, making a note of the date on the Sales/Marketing chart. When payment arrived, I would note that as well as the date of publication. This completed a final transaction.

Eventually, the Baiae story sold twenty-seven times, in eight different countries, and brought in over $10,000. At this point I lost interest in the piece and turned it over to the Canadian syndication outfit, Articles International, with which I have a working agreement. In my cover letter, I provided a list of rights that had been sold to date. Because my focus is primarily on English-language rights, Articles International frequently sells translations of my work to clients in Asia, Europe, and South America.

There are many factors that play into your business success or failure. Among these are the time and effort required for each project and your ability to maximize the sale of your final product. To ensure your success, you should use what I call "MTMS" theory. That is "Minimum Time and Maximum Sales." The global marketing technique outlined above is a blueprint for this. By following this example, you will be able to extend your article sales—spending perhaps 50 percent of your time on marketing and the other half on actual writing.

Another step toward the MTMS goal is the immediate follow-up of article sales. When editors purchase your work, they are basically saying, "We like your style and material." It therefore goes without saying that, with the right idea, you can easily sell to them again. Too often, however, writers simply move on to other projects, seeking new markets, without asking themselves the question, "What else can I sell to *this* publication?"

The key is to strike while the fire is still hot. Just last week I lost a $350 sale of an article, which was already written, because I failed to act quickly. I'd sold a travel story to Army Times Publishing Company and, following the sale, made a note to query the editor on another subject. Two months later I got around to sending the e-mail query. Her reply: "I wish you'd have sent this last month, because I really like the idea. We recently purchased a piece from the same geographical area, however, and as a result I must say no."

A day late, a dollar short.

I've experienced great success with multiple-idea queries following the publication of an initial feature. Once a story appears in print, images are returned, and a check is received, I immediately try to send a thank-you letter to the editor. Conveniently, the thank you also acts as a cover letter for a two-page list of ideas. Each idea consists of a title and a one-paragraph overview of the proposed article, including word length and availability of photographs. Several years ago, this technique won over Carl Beibom, then editor of Scandinavian Airlines' in-flight magazine, *Scanorama*.

I had sold Beibom an in-depth feature on jellyfish. Upon publication, I sent him a standard thank-you letter and added, "With hopes that we might work together on other projects, I am taking advantage of this correspondence to include a list of article ideas for your consideration." The two additional pages included seven topics, from which

Beibom selected volcano exploring and icebergs as my next assignments. I ultimately became a regular contributor to *Scanorama,* selling six or more articles a year.

Some of the best sales tools I have found—though one writers frequently overlook—are special days, weeks, and months. Practically every publication focusing on couples and families, or targeted specifically to the female or male markets, will have a Valentine's Day story in February. The guerrilla marketer goes beyond the obvious, however. You might point out to editors that February is also Vegetarian Month, American History Month, Black History Month, and Celebration of Chocolate Month. Further investigation would also reveal that February contains National Crime Prevention Week, Health Education Week, and Pay Your Bills Week (great for newspaper business sections as well as magazines dealing with the economy).

If you're still stuck for ideas, find out which noted personalities were born during a particular month. Still in February, for instance, you could focus on famous writers: Charles Dickens, Sinclair Lewis, Irwin Shaw, Gertrude Stein, and John Steinbeck were all born that month.

The reason most magazines and newspapers crave special tie-in features is because it offers their advertising departments an excuse to solicit business. Let's say the Sunday supplement of your daily newspaper is running a special edition on Valentine's Day. Because of your wise business sense, you queried the paper—some months in advance—with ideas for a feature on "The Top Ten Valentine's Day Gifts" and a second article on "What Girls Really Want for Valentine's Day." Both ideas were accepted and will appear in the special section.

Based on these features, the soldiers of sales hit the battlefield, taking on local florists, candy and perfume manufacturers, jewelers, restaurants that will be offering

Valentine's Day meals, telephone companies (call someone you love), and even the U.S. Postal Service (send your loved one a special message this Valentine's Day). The bottom line is that the newspaper increases its advertising revenue, the editor gets a pat on the back for being so insightful into the special occasion market, and you become a valued writer.

My suggestion to all writers is to review a copy of *Chase's Annual Events* at the local library and make a list of the special days/weeks/months for which you can come up with tie-in stories. Another option is to visit the events Web site at *http://dailyglobe.com/day2day.html.* Both sources provide thousands of possible article ideas.

Gimmicks

Guerrilla marketing, while calling for innovative techniques and some risk taking, does not mean that one must give up professionalism and quality: These factors will sell more articles than any gimmick or flag waving. Unique marketing tactics will, however, get you more notice than pedestrian strategies and get your materials into the hands of the right people for serious consideration.

I've tried just about every gimmick in the book, some with a high degree of success, others with utter failure. Taking into account the supermarket coupon boom, I tried including a discount coupon in every completed article— 15% OFF YOUR NEXT ARTICLE PURCHASE. I also tried SPECIAL SUMMER SALES or WINTER WRITER'S SALE. Toward the end of the year, there were a few editors who had dwindled their budgets and took advantage of these offers. Most, however, merely viewed this tactic as amateurish and unprofessional. One editor, in fact, told me that he preferred to increase a writer's payment to ensure that he obtained the highest possible quality.

After several years of freelancing, most writers have a stable of editors they sell to—I know I do. To survive as a business, though, your list of buyers must constantly grow, adding new editors and new personalities. At the same time, you must maintain your current customer list.

Exactly what does it mean to "maintain" a customer list? Let's look at it this way: You've spent a great deal of time and effort building a relationship with editors across the country or around the world. In many cases, they've become friends. Communication is one of the main links to any friendship. Remember your classmates from high school or college? Why have most if not all of them faded out of your life? Lack of communication. The same is true with editors. If you do not consistently keep your name in front of them, your spot on their "preferred writers" list will eventually be filled by someone else, perhaps even me.

It was the summer of 1995 when I first felt that I was losing contact with certain editors. One of the reasons was that my list of clients had grown so large that individual communications became impossible. At the same time, however, I knew that there was work to be had from those on my list. It was then that the concept of a newsletter came to mind.

For five years, I had been publishing the *Markets Abroad* newsletter for freelance writers and photographers. Slowly I was moving this venture into the electronic age after realizing the ease and cost-effectiveness of publishing by e-mail. So why not take advantage of Internet technology to maintain contact with clients? In short, produce and electronically distribute a sales letter.

The first issue of *Covering the World with Michael Sedge* went out in October of 1995. In addition to an introductory letter—written as if I were writing to a friend—the newsletter contained a list of article ideas called "On the Writing

Board." These were proposed as features I would be producing in the coming year, and contained an invitation to each recipient to request any or all of these for publishing consideration. There was also a section titled "Travels with Mike," under which I listed blurbs of upcoming trips. At the end of each listing, I wrote, "To obtain a feature specifically focused and written for your readership, send your e-mail requests to Mike at *pp10013@cybernet.it.*"

Because of its friendly style, the premier issue of *Covering the World with Michael Sedge* took only two days to produce—it was only four pages—and distribute by e-mail. The flood of requests it generated took an entire year to fulfill. By Christmas, I had a list of twenty-one assignments that stretched from January through December of the following year. Best of all, nearly all the editors—even if they did not take advantage of my offers—sent a reply saying that it was nice to hear from me and that I should keep in touch. I had thus achieved my goal of "maintaining" my customer list while increasing my annual revenue from article sales.

One thing that will definitely increase your sales is to provide a total package—meaning photography, graphics, and text. When speaking with freelance writers, I hear a lot of whining when I mention photographs. Truth is, there are thousands of sources that will provide tons of free images for the asking. Let's imagine you are working on a general interest story about joining an archaeological expedition. During your research, you will no doubt come up with numerous sources for free pictures. Some of these might be the PR departments of universities and museums. Then there are specialized adventure travel companies, such as Mountain Travel Sobek, that will provide you with images of their tours. Then there are the tourist bureaus. And don't forget the press offices of television stations like the Discovery Channel that run regular documentaries on excavation adventures.

That's fine, you say, for a piece on archaeology. But what if you are writing about flowers? Try the manufacturers of seeds, visit your local flower shop, and contact the media department of FTD Florists. As I said, there are free picture sources for every need. All it takes is a little thinking, a little research, and a little extra effort. In the long run, though, increased sales and a little extra in the paycheck will reward such work.

In my experience, more often than not, editors will pay a writer for images, even if they've been obtained from PR sources. As one editor told me, "I am happy to pay a writer for photographs we use, because of the time and effort they have saved me searching for images."

Operating a stock photo agency for many years taught me that there are ways for writers who can also provide photographs to greatly increase their income by "writing for the cover." I try to do this at every occasion, and am pleased to report that I succeed in landing between seven and twelve cover stories (and photos) a year. Most recently, for example, my work has adorned the cover of Mobil Oil's *Compass,* Singapore Airport's *Changi,* and *Scientific American Archaeology.*

Making the Cover

The first thing you must realize if you want to produce a cover feature is that it is not the story but the images that determine what lands on the cover. Therefore, it is important to obtain pictures *before* you write, whenever possible. My *Changi* piece was on Milan. I requested images from a variety of sources and, upon receiving them, noted a superb-quality, vertical transparency of the city's picturesque cathedral. The image cried out *cover.* Armed with this, I set out to write a lead that captured that image in words. If successful, I would land the cover. If not, I'd still get a good inside spread. The lead read:

> Reaching to the sky with hundreds of intricate spires of architectural splendor, the Cathedral of Milan is like a great heart maintaining the religious pulse of the city. At every hour of the day and night people flow in and out of the encompassing Piazza Duomo, carrying the life-sustaining energy required to drive this European business, fashion, and cultural center. Mark Twain called the city's cathedral "a poem in marble," while Henry James described Milan as being more "the last of the prose capitals than the first of the poetic."

I was pleased with the lead and the photograph. To ensure that the editor, Claudette Peralta, would be thinking "cover" when she read the story, I included the following line in the letter that accompanied the editorial package:

"I am extremely pleased with the images that accompany the article—particularly the cathedral picture, which would make an excellent Christmas cover."

Some time later, I received a letter from Peralta saying that my story on Milan would appear in the December/ January issue and that payment would soon follow for text, four inside photographs, and one cover picture.

Taking the time to "think" about a cover, "write" for a cover, and "suggest" a cover, increased my payment of this package by $260.

Short and Goal

Early in my writing career, I did a great deal of work for magazines that paid 10¢ a word and sometimes less. While these were excellent stepping-stones toward learning the craft and business of writing, I soon realized that they were futile efforts when it came to earning a living as a freelance writer and practicing successful time management. These publications, however, were much easier to sell to than those paying $1 or more a word. My success rate, in fact, was probably thirty articles accepted by the lower-paying magazines for every one sale to a top market.

Like other writers, I thrilled at seeing my work spread over four to six pages of glossy, magazine print. Unlike many colleagues, though, I quickly realized that visual elegance was not going to pay the gas, the telephone, or the electricity bill—and neither was 10¢ a word. At this point in my career, I was perhaps more fortunate than others because I had the opportunity to collaborate with a veteran travel writer. During the week we spent together, his years of knowledge and wisdom poured out. But it was under a full, July moon, at an open-air café along Rome's Via Veneto, that he revealed his "little secret."

"I haven't written a feature article in three years," he said with a smile of success. "But my annual income has not decreased one penny. You see, Mike, I've been writing shorts. That is, 250- to 500-word pieces. I'd say that 80 percent of today's magazines use short news, humor, and human-interest items. For a lot of editors—including those at top-paying publications—this is an area in which they are desperate for material. That is because writers prefer to produce features. I can put out one or two short items a day, in most cases with very little research. The best part is I normally make $1 a word."

It didn't take much effort to realize that $250 for 250 words was far better than $150 for 1,500 words. And so began my success as a writer of "shorts." This shift in direction also launched my career upward, into markets that I had always sought to write for—*Attenzione, Family Circle, Newsweek, Reader's Digest, Travel and Leisure,* and an array of popular magazines for men.

I still spend at least five to six days each month writing nothing but short items. In fact, I have standing contracts with two editors for such items. Gus Venditto, editor-in-chief of Mecklemedia's *Internet.com*, pays me $600 a month for two 300-word news pieces about Internet development in Italy. The publisher of *Scientific American Archaeology* made me a similar offer, with a $750 price tag. From these two arrangements alone, I am guaranteed $1,350 a month for 1,200 words (better than $1.12 a word). And that is enough to buy a new Saturn each year.

More than this, news items or fillers, as they are frequently called, can lead to larger assignments as well as inside information into editorial needs. Because I know that the editor-in-chief of *Scientific American Archaeology* likes breaking news stories on the cover, I recently suggested a story about a project that would be the focus of an upcoming documentary on the Discovery Channel. As a result, I came away with an assignment to write the story, worth $1,750. Similarly, my work with *Internet.com* landed me an assignment not long ago from another Mecklemedia publication. This job brought in $2,200.

The lesson here is easy to grasp: In your climb to success, don't overlook the market for short articles. This type of work can launch a career into new heights. In your quest, however, seek out those publications that pay well for your efforts. The results can be very lucrative if you do.

SELLING YOURSELF

B y 1982, I had already achieved fair success as a writer for local publications and newspapers. Like thousands of others, however, I entertained visions of bigger and better things, of national publication, of global success, of books, and perhaps even a movie. This was the same year, after a semester of college marketing at the University of La Verne, California, that I began to think of myself as a product.

---

pro•duct *n.* 1. Anything that fills a need or desire and can be offered to a market.

Because a product is generally categorized as an object, a place, an organization, a service, or an idea, you rarely consider a person, let alone yourself, a product. In a marketing sense, however, that is exactly what you must become to achieve commercial success. Granted, as a writer, you will most often be hired for your services—producing press releases, articles, brochures, and books. Or perhaps you will be contracted to teach a writing seminar, or give a lecture. While these are all services you provide, the true product is *you*.

All marketing experts—particularly guerrilla marketers—realize that a successful product must have three primary characteristics. It must first provide a benefit. Second, it must have a brand name that customers recognize. And, third, it must have a guarantee or after-sale satisfaction. How do each of these apply to you? That is the exact question I asked myself in 1982, and what you must ask yourself now. Your immediate reaction, as was mine, might be that you offer no benefit, that no one recognizes your name, and that you cannot provide any form of guarantee. Before jumping to such conclusions, however, let's take a closer look at each of these categories.

What Benefits Do You Provide?

There is a mystique to the writing profession that almost instantly confers upon you a celebrity status. My writing career has gained me invitations to the homes of ambassadors, Hollywood producers, and politicians. It has opened the door to guest spots on television and radio programs. Long before reaching this level, however, I was considered by many to be a local VIP. Why? Because my name regularly appeared in print. I was read and respected by others. What I said influenced people, whether I was reviewing a restaurant or suggesting a low-budget vacation. Quite simply, I had become part of what is commonly termed the "power of the press."

I quickly learned to use—but not abuse—this power to my advantage. When in London, I received complimentary tickets to top musicals, thanks to the PR department of Andrew Lloyd-Webber's production company, The Really Useful Group. In Rome, I dined at La Sans Sausi, the famed hangout of Jackie Onassis. The director of the Philippine National Tourist Office made me his guest in Manila. And I was offered a complimentary helicopter ride over New York City, simply to obtain photographs from a unique angle.

These few examples demonstrate how you and I are different from the rest of the world. We are the press, the media, and the news. In an exaggerated sense, we generate the ideas and concepts that people will discuss over breakfast and dinner. We provide the facts that will alter the decisions of the public. And that makes us unique. That makes us special. That makes us celebrities.

Inasmuch as we can utilize our media status to gain access to spots where the normal citizen cannot go and, as well, can produce articles of various degrees of influence, what real benefits do we—as products—offer?

To answer this question, we need to go back to the essence of guerrilla marketing: filling a need. If you were an editor in need of an article, a writer could certainly be beneficial. If you were a business executive in need of a speech, a presentation, or a corporate report, you would no doubt be looking for a top professional scribe to handle the job. And what about the university administrator who has scheduled a writing seminar? Where does she go for an instructor? Then there is the local Rotary Club; the club needs keynote speakers for each of its monthly meetings. A local writer would fit that bill perfectly. Perhaps you have noticed the increasing number of writers appearing on regional and national television programs in recent years or speaking on the radio about topics on which they have written.

The needs for writers are endless, and so are the benefits you can offer. By marketing yourself, you are offering to fill a need, which grows daily. You are the expert, the celebrity, and the magical person with the ability to take readers to new worlds, to make them laugh, cry, and wonder. Yes, you do offer benefits. Once you realize this, new horizons of opportunity will begin to appear.

But what about name recognition? There are certainly people who have read your works; perhaps you even have a following of readers. If not, don't worry. Name recognition is something you can build. When I began my first "Mike Sedge" marketing campaign, for example, I was literally unknown to all but a few local readers. Within six months, however, I was featured in several business and writer publications, including *Entrepreneur*. Suddenly I was getting letters from former high school friends living thousands of miles away. My relatives began calling me "the celebrity."

As the snowball grew, so did the moneymaking opportunities—teaching, lecturing, contributing editor positions, brochures, and ultimately a corporate media contract resulting in nearly $400,000 over the next six years.

"Don't just toot your horn . . . BLOW the DAMN BUGLE! You may have the most terrific book (or product) ever, but if no one knows about it . . . it won't sell."

—*Jan Larkey, writer, speaker, consultant*

Name recognition is a matter of perspective as much as it is a matter of position or status. To illustrate this, take a look at the following names and see how many you recognize:

1. Bill Gates
2. John Hendricks

3. Madeleine K. Albright
4. Mary Ann Elliott
5. Norman H. Schwarzkopf, Jr.
6. T. Joseph Lopez
7. Stephen King
8. Frances Mayes
9. Steven Spielberg
10. Jeffrey Katzenberg

If you are like most people, you guessed all the odd numbers: 1, 3, 5, 7, 9. And, yet, the people listed next to the even numbers hold as much prestige as those by the odd numbers. In fact, they hold very similar positions. While Bill Gates is CEO of Microsoft Corp., John Hendricks is founder and CEO of Discovery Communications, Inc. (the Discovery Channel). Mary Ann Elliott, CEO of Arrowhead Space and Telecommunications, Inc., was recently nominated as one of Washington's most influential people, along with U.S. Secretary of State, Madeleine K. Albright. We all know General Norman Schwarzkopf from the Gulf War, but how many recognize Admiral T. Joseph Lopez, former commander in chief of Allied Forces Southern Europe during the war in Bosnia? Author Steven King, at number 7, is the Edgar Allan Poe of the twentieth century. But did you know the author of the bestsellers *Under the Tuscan Sun* and *Bella Tuscany,* Frances Mayes? If you answered yes, I congratulate you. If you said no, it might surprise you to know that *Under the Tuscan Sun* was on the national bestseller list for nearly two years, and *Bella Tuscany* rose to the rank of bestseller as soon as it was published in 1999. Finally, we come to Spielberg and Katzenberg. No doubt 75 percent of the U.S. population recognizes the director of *Jaws, E.T.,* and *Schindler's List,* but perhaps only 2 percent know who the latter is. They are, however, partners in the film production company Dreamworks SKG.

So why do people recognize Spielberg but not Katzenberg, or King and not Mayes? Very simply, because the even-numbered individuals are not in the media spotlight. For the most part, they do not appear on global television, they do not do national radio interviews, and they are not featured in major publications, while their counterparts are. As a result, Bill Gates and Schwarzkopf have become household names.

Writers can learn to build name recognition simply by taking advantage of media opportunities—sometimes even creating them. In addition, you can enhance your name— even if you are unknown—by associating it with companies that you have worked for or have some connection with. In a cover letter or press release, for example, I could easily present myself as follows:

> Michael Sedge, a twenty-year veteran journalist, has worked for many of today's top media. As a member of the American Society of Journalists and Authors, Sedge has published more than 2,600 articles and several books. He is an editor for *Scientific American Archaeology* and has been featured in many magazines and newspapers.

There is nothing wrong with this presentation. It's to the point, highlights my longstanding professionalism and reliability as a writer, and indicates prestige by including *Scientific American Archaeology*. Look at how much greater the presentation becomes, however, by dropping names:

> Michael Sedge is a twenty-year veteran journalist, with more than 2,600 articles and several books to his credit, including the award-winning *Commercialization of the Oceans* (Franklin Watts). His global clientele includes The Associated Press, *Newsweek,* the Discovery

Channel, and Time-Life Books. Recently hired by *Scientific American Archaeology* as Mediterranean and Middle East editor, Mr. Sedge has been called "the wizard of marketing" by *Entrepreneur* magazine.

In this single paragraph, I've suddenly generated name recognition. Not because a potential client would know *me*, but because I associate myself with world-famous names such as *Newsweek*, the Discovery Channel, and *Scientific American*. I could just as easily say, *Going Places Doing Things, The New Entertainer, R&R Magazine*, or *Tropi-Ties*. But other than a very limited readership, who knows these publications? In fact, including these lesser-known names in my short bio would achieve just the opposite of what I want. It would lead prospective clients to ask, "What are these publications, and who is this guy?"

I even go one step further in my quest for name recognition by including a quote from *Entrepreneur*. Reading this, a potential client might say to himself, "Wow, this guy has been around. I can't believe I've never heard of him!"

And this is exactly what you want him to be thinking: "I'd really like to get this guy to be a guest speaker, an instructor, a writer for our magazine, or a staff journalist. But can we afford him?"

Fortunately, I've been able to weasel myself into these positions several times, and so can you. In most cases, the results are steady, well-paying jobs. In some cases, the potential client was right—he could not afford me. My goal in this chapter is to get you thinking about self-promotion, as well as providing insight that will lead to name-recognition opportunities.

First, however, let's explore the last area that would qualify you to be considered a "product." That is, what guarantee can you offer? The Mike Sedge bio above immediately indicates that I am reliable and, thus, implies a guarantee to anyone who hires me. The fact that you have past credentials is insurance that you can and will complete a job in a professional manner—whether it is a speaking engagement, teaching a writing course, or writing a speech for a local politician. Your reputation, in other words, is your guarantee.

A writer who does not meet deadlines, does not show up for appointments, does not provide a high-quality service or product will soon be weeded out from the garden of productive professionals. Why? Because she cannot offer the guarantee that clients must have in order to hire her. Can you imagine going to a car dealer and ordering a new vehicle with no assurance of a date when it will be delivered? No doubt, you would go to another dealer. The same is true for your clients.

What's in a Name?

The first step in self-promotion, or selling yourself, is mindset. You cannot simply sit down and say, "Well, today I guess I'll put myself on the auction block." It doesn't work that way. Just as *The Making of a President* illustrated the activities that go on behind the "selling" of a presidential candidate, you must concentrate on day-to-day marketing efforts that generate media coverage. This, in turn, will make your name known locally, regionally, and nationally.

Let's imagine, for example, that I am a local politician. A friend has suggested that I contact you because of your professionalism, media contacts, and ability to write truthful, yet positive profiles. We set up a meeting and during our discussion, I point out that I want a media kit containing the following items:

- a press release highlighting my career
- a feature article highlighting one or more aspects of my professional activities

- a list of questions and answers for possible interviews
- a professional-quality, 5 × 7–inch color portrait
- news clips that cast me and my career in the best light

You think about it for a while, then accept the job. Now imagine that *you* are that politician. This client-employee relationship is the mindset you must have in order to do justice to your self-marketing. Your editorial business is now the PR firm and you are the client. This campaign is not *The Making of a President* but *The Making of (your name)*.

"Inasmuch as writers are responsible for all news media, it is amazing how few know how to utilize it to their advantage."

—*Joel Jacobs, thirty-year veteran journalist*

There are two forms of media exposure: advertising and promotion. The distinction between the two is quite simple: You pay for the first, the second is free. I don't know why any writer would ever advertise, though I have known some who did—with very little success, I might add. What you want is free promotion. You want articles about yourself to appear in as many media outlets as possible, you want to appear on television, you want to be a guest on radio shows, you want to be invited to talk to groups. The more exposure you get, the more work you will receive.

During the 1980s, veteran travel writer Bern Keating and I were collaborating on a series of audiotapes covering Italian walking tours for Tape Guide, Inc. One day I asked Bern, "How did you get involved in this project?"

"I'd been invited to talk about travel writing at an ASJA meeting. After the lecture, the owner of Tape Guide came up to me and offered the job."

A press kit, or media kit as they are sometimes referred to, is the first step in your promotional efforts. Just as the politician needed a press release, a feature article, a list of questions and answers, and a photo in his kit, so will you. These are the standard items and, most often, fill the needs of any editor or producer receiving it. A business card should also be added, in the event that additional information or interviews need to be arranged.

If your business is established under a name other than yours, it will be much easier to produce a credible media kit. If not, make sure that your name is presented as a company, rather than a person. For example, John Smith & Associates or John Smith Company. Then, when you produce press releases, you become John Smith, founder and CEO of John Smith & Associates.

It's the big name game all over again. Another option would be to come up with a brand name for such activities. A brand can be any name, symbol, or logo used in selling a product or service. You may be operating as Ellen Epstein, freelance writer. For your press kit, you might select a brand name of EE Editorial. In the past I've utilized such brands as Michael Sedge & Associates, The Sedge Group, Medusa Photos, and 3 Kings Communications. In each case I designed a logo based on the brand title and used it on the cover of media kits as well as stationery and business cards.

"Most of my work is now done under contract to organizations, including professional associations, government agencies, and businesses . . . I rely on visibility to keep my name afloat. Thus, I am active in my local professional associations, give a lot of speeches on what it is I do . . . write occasional articles for professional publications, and also teach in a highly respected publications specialist program."

—*Shirley Sirota Rosenberg, professional writer*

The important factor to remember is that you have to distance yourself from the media kit presentation—in the eyes of the client. This means never use "I" in the press release or article, unless used in a quote, and never use your own name as a contact point or to sign cover letters. There are ways to get around this, even though you may be a one-person operation. I utilize my Strawberry Media presentation folders for all press kits, along with the company stationery. Additionally, I have business cards printed for Gabriella Giugliano (my wife), and I have given her a title for this purpose—public relations manager. Her name goes on all cover letters and she is listed as "point of contact" for additional information.

Distancing yourself makes everything more professional, more "big league." If you were requesting information about John Hendricks, founder and CEO of the Discovery Channel, would you expect to receive it directly from Hendricks? Of course not; he is much to busy for that. The company has a public relations office for such things. This is the exact image you want to present for your business. You are the Big Cheese, the Grand Swiss, and, below you, are the Tiny Cheddars doing your PR. Having an executive image will also make potential clients want you that much more. It's just human nature: Everyone desires things that are difficult or impossible to have.

Creating Your Kit

The first line of attack in self-marketing is a press release. A good release is the secret to getting media attention and your name in the public eye. For many writers, a press release is something you create after publishing a book. Granted, authoring a book is an excellent, newsworthy excuse for sending out such notices. Guerrilla marketers, however, don't sit around waiting for such obvious opportunities.

They create their own news. They are constantly thinking of reasons for an editor or producer to mention them, to invite them to speak, to have them as guests on their programs.

I've written hundreds of press releases, many of which spotlighted me and my work. Without flooding the market, I try to put out a notice that will generate name recognition and/or increase my clientele every other month. Here are some of the titles of my non-book-related releases:

- Local Writer Teams Up with the Discovery Channel
- Sedge Nominated Regional President of IFW&TWA
- Marketing Wizard Targets U.S. Military
- NATO Commander Honors Peacekeeping Writer
- Expert on Global Marketing Releases New Book
- Italian Fashions, through American Eyes
- Sunken City Found off Egyptian Coast
- ASJA Opens European/Middle East Chapter

I utilized my assignment for the Discovery Channel to "make news" about myself in local newspapers and city magazines. By associating myself with the popular television network, I was instantly categorized as a celebrity and, therefore, made the local entertainment sections. In the second release, I used my nomination to the regional presidency of the International Food, Wine and Travel Writers Association to gain exposure in both travel and gastronomy publications. Because I also sent this release to TV and radio stations, I was asked to be a guest on a television program about Italian cuisine.

"Marketing Wizard Targets U.S. Military." This headline, followed by a 224-word news story about my efforts in media geared to service members, led to *Entrepreneur* magazine featuring me in a two-page spread, with a color photo. *Entrepreneur* utilized nearly the exact wording in my release, calling me the "Wizard of Marketing." This, in turn, brought me the best-paying, long-term corporate contract I have ever had. It also generated several speaking engagements and opened the door to other marketing opportunities. The article appeared more than eight years ago, and I am still reaping the benefits. In fact, just five minutes ago, I received a call from Bob Helms, assistant advertising director at *European Stars and Stripes.* He asked, "Are you still writing and doing military marketing?" Naturally, I said yes. "Great. I am going to give your name and phone number to a businessman in London. He is looking to contract someone to boost his sales in this market. I figured with your experience and media contacts, you would be the perfect person."

I can't wait for the call!

Each of the other press releases focused on some aspect of the work I was doing at that time. When I covered fashion, I sent a release out to the top magazines in that sector. After writing a feature about NATO commander, Admiral T. Joseph Lopez, I was presented with an award for excellence in journalism. This was a worthy news topic for both international newspapers and trade magazines.

The closer you can link your press release to a news topic, the greater your chances of coverage. Using recently published articles is a good way to become an instant expert on a subject—particularly if your goal is to get on television or radio shows. Say you've written a piece for *Travel-Holiday* on "The Perfect Honeymoon Spots." This is an excellent topic for talk shows and, because you've done all the research and published the results in a national magazine, you are the perfect candidate to discuss it. You might even go one step further and ask the publication's sales or marketing staff if they would like to participate in a cooperative effort. In this case, they pay for the printing and mailing of the press releases in exchange for the magazine being mentioned.

During the past month, several magazine editors and writers have appeared on NBC's *Today* show discussing various topics—health, money, aging, and the like. In nearly every case, the host says, "You can obtain more information on this topic in the next issue of *XYZ Magazine*." For guerrilla writers, there is a very important underlying message in that phrase. It tells you to get a press release out to media sources as soon as you have an assignment from a major magazine. Why? Because it allows producers to schedule you as a guest at the same time that the article appears. This, in turn, provides an opportunity to get the magazine involved. The exposure will create greater sales of the publication and, as well, will enhance advertising sales of the magazine—and will certainly help you gain future article assignments.

If you are unfamiliar with press release formats, you'll want to take note of the sample below. Always provide a point of contact for additional information. List a telephone number and, if you have a fax, your fax number as well. You should also include an e-mail address. To maintain your "big company" image, I suggest establishing a free e-mail account with Yahoo.com, Hotmail.com, or any of the other Internet companies offering such service. For example, I often use *SMEDIAPR@yahoo.com*. Anyone receiving the release might therefore think that it came from the Strawberry Media Public Relations Department. That is exactly what I want them to think.

Your release should also contain a date or the words FOR IMMEDIATE RELEASE. If the information is time sensitive, you should state, "NOT TO BE RELEASED UNTIL (date)." A good example of time sensitive material is the annual list of "The Most Boring Celebrities of the Year," put out by writer and marketing whiz Alan Caruba. While he wants the release to be in the hands of editors and producers, he also wants a simultaneous distribution of the information, resulting in a media blitz. To achieve this, Caruba specifies a date when the press release can be used.

Contact:
Gabriella Giugliano
Public Relations Manager
Tel. (39) 081-851-2208
Fax. (39) 081-851-2210
E-mail: SMEDIAPR@yahoo.com   FOR IMMEDIATE RELEASE

NATO COMMANDER HONORS PEACE-KEEPING WRITER

Naples, Italy—Admiral Jack Sampson, Commander-in-Chief, Allied Forces Southern Europe, honored American writer Michael Sedge today for his professionalism and reporting of positive, humanitarian aspects during the recent conflict in the former Yugoslavian territory of Bosnia.

"If there were a rose growing in a junkyard, Sedge would find it and report its beauty," said Sampson. "This is what makes his journalism unique—heart-warming. Our goal, as military leaders, is not to fight wars, but to maintain peace. If more journalists took the example of Michael Sedge, our job would be much easier."

During the ceremony, attended by military leaders from various Southern European NATO commands, Sedge was awarded a certificate and meritorious medal for journalistic excellence. It was the first time such an award has been given to a writer.

"Too often, world media plays a negative role in conflicts such as Bosnia," explained Sedge, a native of Flint, Michigan. "Behind the scenes, there are humanitarian efforts taking place that are rarely seen or recognized. I consider it my responsibility to point these efforts out. Others will provide the details of daily conflicts and body counts."

The award was specifically given for Sedge's article in *Diplomat* magazine, published in the United Kingdom. The story, titled "Four Star Peacekeeper," highlighted the efforts of Admiral T. Joseph Lopez, former Commander of NATO peace-keeping forces in Bosnia. Now retired and living in Arlington, Virginia, Lopez said it was one of the finest articles ever published on the efforts to maintain stability in this war zone.

Sedge, who heads the global editorial agency, Strawberry Media, has covered U.S. and NATO military affairs in the Mediterranean and Middle East for nearly twenty years. His clients have included The Associated Press, *Armed Forces Journal International, Army Times,* and *Newsweek.* Author of several books, Sedge recently worked as a special assignment writer in Alexandria, Egypt, for the Discovery Channel. His Internet website can be found at *www.cybernet.it/sedge.*

Strawberry Media

Europe: Via Venezia 14/b * 80021 Afragola (NA) Italy
USA: 2733 Midland Road * Shelbyville, TN * USA

Editors and producers are busy people. I, therefore, try to make their jobs easier by "slapping" News Releases in their faces in bold type. That immediately tells them that this information is free, and if they want their story to be different than those appearing in competing publications, they can call the contact point and get additional information or quotes—even set up an interview, if they'd like. This is the reason I highlight the words "News Release" and ensure that the point of contact information is at the top of the page.

In the headline you should always try to illustrate a benefit—the editor's, the producer's, the reader's, and even your own. In this case, I've provided the recipients with a new and unique angle to an old story—the war in Bosnia. For the reader I offer a human-interest aspect. And what's in it for me? The release, when published, offers new opportunities for business as well as exposure and name recognition. Say the editor of *Armed Forces Journal International (AFJI)* is looking for a correspondent in the Mediterranean. Reading this news item in a newspaper in Washington—where *AFJI* is based—he might immediately consider me for the job. (This actually happened, by the way, and I am now a foreign correspondent for *AFJI*.) Or suppose a producer, receiving this release in a press kit, is looking for a talk show guest to discuss the conflict in Iraq. Suddenly, I am a candidate, given my credentials and recent award. Then, to go one step further, let's say the show is *Good Morning America* and that a book publisher is sipping coffee and watching the show before heading out to fight Big Apple traffic. He's been giving some thought to putting out a title on military activities in the Gulf, but hasn't been able to come up with a writer. Then, there I am—his writer, his expert. Ready, willing, and able—if the price is right, of course.

This is the snowball effect that press releases and continuous media coverage can create for writers. This is also the reason that the most popular and successful writers in America are constantly appearing on TV, radio, and in the print media.

Always use the body of your press release to provide credibility. Who you are, what you've done. And remember to drop names of your important clients. For this release, I've linked myself with admirals Sampson and Lopez, thereby riding their coattails.

Finally, provide a source for readers to obtain more information. Include telephone and fax numbers, e-mail and postal addresses, and, if you have one, a Web site where potential clients will find more details. If you are selling a book or other product, this would also be the place to include ordering information.

Generally, press releases should be no more than two pages. Always try to come up with a news slant, if possible, and, as with all hard copy for media use, double space all releases.

In your press kit, you might include an article about yourself or some aspect of your business. This could enhance the chances of your gaining media coverage. If you target the market correctly—just as you would to sell them an article—the editor may publish your piece exactly as written. More often than not, though, an associate editor will rewrite the article. To promote my last book, *The Writer's and Photographer's Guide to Global Markets,* I prepared a feature on selling articles around the world. It was published, as presented, on the Internet site *Writing Now.* Other publications for writers, including *Authorlink, Inklings,* and *National Writers Monthly* ran altered versions of the story. Based on my initial material, another popular Web site, *Writer On Line,* assigned a contributing editor to write a major feature on my international sales activities. This ultimately led to them contracting me to write the monthly "Going Global with Mike Sedge" column.

In some cases, an article can be substituted for a one-page biography. I will frequently send media kits to editors if I am seeking to land a contributing editor position. If you are hoping to land a corporate account, however, a biography of your professional credits would be more appropriate than an article, which is primarily aimed at media outlets.

Because press releases and articles included in your press kit will often stimulate additional questions from editors, producers, or others who receive the package, it is always a good idea to include one or two pages of questions and answers. Naturally, these should be focused on the general theme you are trying to convey with the package. For instance, when I wanted to promote my book on international marketing, the questions I included focused on how writers and photographers could find global markets, the types of material that sells best to foreign editors, what you can expect to be paid, and so on.

On the other hand, if my press kit spotlighted a military topic—such as the Iraq conflict—I might include questions and answers dealing with the effects of world media on military efforts, the hazards of being a war correspondent, a comparison of military strengths, and perhaps a statement spelling out the disparate political views of the conflict.

Because press releases should go to broadcast as well as print media, including a question and answer sheet will give producers of TV and radio talk shows some idea of the responses you might give if you were asked to be a guest. In fact, the questions asked by show hosts are frequently those included in an initial media kit. Why? Because producers are fairly certain of your replies and can avoid any radical surprises.

You should always include a 5 × 7–inch, or larger, color photo of yourself. As with every aspect of your business, you'll want your photo to be as professional as possible. Don't try to get away with an instant, photo-booth snapshot, or a cut-and-paste portrait from a summer beach picture. Take the time and invest the money to go to a professional photo studio. Explain to the photographer that the images will be used in a press kit, and get some top-of-the-line portrait shots. Don't be afraid to be creative. In some pictures, you might want to include a typewriter, a computer, some of your published work, or anything else that might symbolize your business.

A good picture provides a double benefit. First, it offers an illustration for print media. Second, if you are sending out information to television producers, it gives them an opportunity to see that you do not resemble Frankenstein and, therefore, will not frighten their viewers.

Finally, you may want to include other information in your media kit. For instance, many writers, particularly if they're sending the kit to potential nonmedia clients—for example, corporations or schools—will include clips of published work. For this, always use color copies to highlight your work at its best. If you are trying to land a radio or TV guest spot, you might provide a one-page pitch. If you have recently published an article on bird songs, you might suggest to the radio producer that you could bring along recordings that can be inserted into the program. Or maybe you wrote a how-to piece on growing new plants from stem cuttings. Suggest to a television producer that you could illustrate the various steps involved in this cultivating technique, providing an attractive presentation for viewers. These are the types of things that should go into a pitch letter.

My media kits also contain one page of testimonials—that is, what people or publications have said about me. These one-line comments, much like references listed on a résumé, aid in building credibility, establish professionalism, and indicate what clients you have worked for and how they received your work. Here are some of the more common quotes I use:

> "(Sedge's) work is excellent."—J. Randall, Editor, Mobil Oil *Compass*

> "You are a valuable asset to our organization." —R. Slocum, MCI Communications

> "You are one of the finest and most professional journalists I have ever worked with."—A. Valenti, Articles International

> "Michael Sedge is a mail order genius."—*Income Opportunities*

> "Sedge is the Wizard of marketing."—*Entrepreneur*

> "A true professional."—Jeff Herman, The Jeff Herman Literary Agency

> "There is no one I know who has so many unique and fresh ideas as Mike Sedge."—Joel E. Jacobs, Editor, *The World of Beer*

> "An expert marketer."—Dan Poynter, Para Publishing

Your entire package, when completed, should include a catchy cover letter. Remember: This should come from, and be signed by, your "public relations manager" and not you. Good cover letters will sell the editor, the producer, the executive, and the school administrator, and entice them into looking at the enclosed materials. It will explain why you, your product, your services, or your message is valuable to them and their readers/viewers. In my cover letters, I like to pose a question and then answer it—with statistics whenever possible. Here are a couple of examples:

> "Why are more than 70 percent of today's freelance writers and photographers working at poverty level? Because they are thinking as writers and not marketers."

> "While live war coverage may increase the number of CNN viewers, does it also have an effect on military strategy? The answer, according to top Pentagon officials, is yes!"

Wording like this not only leads to your message but also captures readers, making them ask more questions and seek additional answers. If I were an editor reading the first sentence, I might ask, "Well, why don't they think globally?" When reading the second example, I immediately question *how* it affects military strategy and *who* at the Pentagon says so. In short, I want more—and that will stimulate me to dig into the press kit.

With all the elements packaged in a presentation folder, you now have a media kit. Now what? Where does it go?

Where Does It Go From Here?

There are innumerable target markets for a press kit. Some of these include editors, producers, and corporate executives. Getting media exposure is much like selling an article. You must target the information in your media kit to fit the needs of both the market and yourself. Let's return for a moment to our plant propagation writer. If you recall, she's the one who published a story on raising new plants from stem cuttings. With the proper press release, a copy of the article, a question and answer sheet, and a biography, your PR manager—that is, you—could easily pitch her as a talk show guest to television producers. In this case, the media kit should go out to people like Barbara Fight or JoAnne Salzman, producers of *Live with Regis and Kathie Lee,* or Mary Alice O'Rourke, supervising producer of NBC's *Today.*

"(We like) using authors as experts," explains Stephen McCain, associate producer with CBS-TV's *48 Hours.* "If we're doing a show on celebrity stalkers, we might have someone on to talk about the things people can do to lower the risk of getting in harm's way, or someone who's written a book on alcohol abuse in teenagers if we're doing a show on teen drinking."

Authors Katie and Gene Hamilton took advantage of television and radio to propel their writing on home improvement into a full-time, profitable career. They are currently writing four books, including *Home Improvement for Dummies*. They also write a weekly "Do It Yourself or Not?" column, syndicated nationally by the *Los Angeles Times*.

"We became comfortable doing television and radio interviews a long time ago and have been frequent spokesmen for companies with home improvement products. So promoting our books, newspaper column, and Web site have been very easy and lucrative."

The Hamiltons also introduced the Internet site House Net, *www.housenet.com*, with Katie as the creative director and Gene in the technical director slot. R. R. Donnelley & Sons later acquired the site with the agreement that the writing team stay on as employees.

"What we have always done and continue to do is build our reputation as accomplished and reliable writers about our subject," says Katie. "We've found that parlaying our writing expertise to editors of all varieties and manufacturers in our field has been successful."

This morning, while driving to the airport, I tuned into National Public Radio's *Morning Edition*. The host was discussing stock trading on the Internet. "For more information on this subject," he said, "we have with us Jeffrey Smith, a correspondent for *Business Week*, who has written an article on home trading in the latest issue of the magazine."

This was a perfect example of how writers—even if they only do articles—are making their way into the public eye (or in this case, ear). You no longer have to be the author of a best-selling novel to interest television and radio producers in your topics. All you need are good researching skills, knowledge of your subject, and a well-presented feature story. Oh, yes, and an ability to not choke up in front of the camera or microphone.

"Talk is hot, whether it's on the radio, TV, or Internet," explains Marilyn Ross. She and her husband, Tom, are cofounders of the Small Publishers Association of North America and authors of *Jump-Start Your Book Sales* (see the appendix). "In 1983 there were only fifty-three radio stations with news/talk formats. The February 1998 issue of *American Demographics* reports that there are more than one thousand today!"

Most radio talk show hosts conduct telephone interviews, thus eliminating the need for you to go to the studio. To help writers take full advantage of radio opportunities, Marilyn and Tom Ross offer the following tips:

1. As soon as the phone rings, assume you're on the air. This won't usually be true, since the producer typically comes on first, but you never know when your comments will be broadcast live.
2. Try to listen to the station and show ahead of time. If it's out of your area, one idea is to call the station and ask to be placed on hold: You'll hear the show airing!
3. When you have a guest spot booked in a specific area, check with a couple of local independent bookstores (if you are promoting a book) and tell them that if they order twelve copies or more, you'll plug those stores on the air. Of course, if it's an area show, you should be alerting all bookstores in the vicinity that they will have an increased demand for the book.
4. If you're offering a demo tape, don't send it to a station in the same area. Nobody likes to be a runner-up. Producers prefer exclusives in big markets.
5. Stand and deliver. When you do an interview from a chair, you're slouched and your diaphragm is

scrunched. Stand. Walk. Pace. You'll sound more dynamic. You may want to install a longer phone cord to allow for this flexibility.

6. Relate your book (or other product, including yourself) to newspaper headlines. Maybe you have an alternative viewpoint. Attack the commonly held notion. Explode a myth.

7. You may want to "plant" friends or loved ones to get the call-in ball rolling. Coach them with a leading question.

8. Remember that radio producers and hosts talk . . . to each other. There are sites on the Internet, such as Bit Board and Morning Mouth—closed to the general public—where they gab about outstanding guests. They also have conversations where they network. Be outstanding and they will seek you out like butterflies quest after nectar.

9. Always be on your best vocal behavior. You are "auditioning" from the moment you open your mouth. Think a producer is calling just to check that detail? Nope. He or she wants to hear your voice inflection, how enthusiastic you sound, if you're quick on the mental uptake, and so on. Same thing when you call them. Turn on the charm.

(Reprinted from SPAN Connection,
with permission of the authors)

I use two sources for up-to-date lists and information on television and radio talk shows, though there are numerous others. The first is *Bradley's Guide to the Top National TV Talk Shows*. The second is *Book Marketing Update* (see the appendix). The latter is a twice-a-month newsletter, perfect for keeping larger directories updated.

Print Media

Focusing on topics that fit a particular publication or market is the best way to gain print media coverage. A few years back I began marketing and selling my own book. In my case, it was *The Adventure Guide to Italy.* To minimize my effort and maximize my return, I also began selling other travel titles by the same publisher, Hunter Publishing. This was done under a "drop shipment" system. I handled the marketing, orders came to my office, with payment, and I then forwarded them to Hunter. My return was 50 percent of the profit.

Next I turned this concept into a press release and, along with the standard media kit, sent it to the editor of *Income Opportunities* magazine. The result was a two-and-a-half page article focusing on me and Strawberry Media, including a quarter-page photo. The title of the article was "Overnight Mail Order Success: Drop Shipment."

"I think it's important for writers to market themselves as 'experts' on specific subjects and topics. To this end, I advertise in the *Yearbook of Experts, Authorities and Spokespersons*—Broadcast Interview Source, Washington, D.C.—which includes an index of those areas of expertise I want to emphasize. The *Yearbook* also ensures that I am continually interviewed by both print and broadcast media outlets, not just in the United States, but internationally."

—*Alan Caruba, professional writer and marketing expert*

On another occasion, after spending two weeks in my summer apartment in Florida, I prepared a press kit slanted toward my success as a writer and the rewards of being the owner of timeshare property. It was immediately picked up by *Holiday,* the magazine of RCI timeshare owners, and run on one page with a color photo of my wife and myself. The subtitle of the article read, "Who better to tell how timeshare ownership and exchange makes for better holidays than an RCI member? Freelance journalist and author Michael Sedge, who has published more than 2,500 articles and several books including *The Adventure Guide to Italy,* shares his experience of owning at Vistana Resort, Lake Buena Vista, Florida."

The more exposure you receive—whether it be on television, radio, and the Internet or in the print media—the greater your writing opportunities will be. Your goal should be not only to generate additional income, but to raise yourself to celebrity status. You might begin with a news blurb in a hometown newspaper and a speaking engagement at the local library. No matter how small or large, your self-promotion efforts must be consistent in order to pay off. As Robyn Spizman, author of sixty-three books and a television reporter for WXIA-TV in Atlanta, points out, you must rethink your attitude. Don't feel uncomfortable blowing your own horn. Someone needs the information you possess and using the media is the best way to get it out there.

An area where some writers fall short is in the followup of press kits. Two weeks after you've sent out your packages, call or e-mail anyone who has not replied to ensure that the material arrived. Ask if the recipient would like additional information or a personal meeting to "further explore possible cooperation." There have been occasions when I was required to follow up with editors and producers three or four times before achieving any results. After a while, I believe, they agreed to cover what I was trying to promote simply to get me off their backs—whatever it takes!

For most writers, self-promotion and marketing ultimately leads to nonwriting jobs such as teaching and lecturing. If this is where your interests lie, you can apply a guerrilla marketing approach to such activities. That, and more, can be found in the next chapter.

18 Ways to Promote Yourself and Your Business

by Maggie Klee Lichtenberg © 1999

1. Start with a change you'll need to make if you plan to be successful: Get over being shy.

2. Have the mindset to *consistently* take initiatives. Never stop: It's not enough to create one brilliant direct mail campaign. Repeat the mailing to your list two or three times. And never, never, *never* take an initiative without following up.

3. Plan one marketing effort each day. Every Sunday evening or Monday morning, choose a theme for your week and mark that theme in your calendar each day for the coming week.

4. Develop a PR plan for you *and* your company. Work with a publicist (or do your own PR) to land features and interviews. Create a sample press kit that contains your mission statement, a warm and friendly letter including company bio, press coverage, personal testimonials, and a professional black-and-white photo of you.

5. Show up a lot—be *seen*. Tell everyone what you're up to. Always have a book, a press kit, a flyer about your company ready to give away.

6. Have a short, laser-sharp intro about yourself—twenty words or less—ready to go at all times. Be a graceful, yet tireless, self-promoter.

7. Commit to public speaking. Join a Toastmasters group for six months to increase confidence. Build positive relationships with everyone you meet.

8. Create an audiotape business card and give it away. This is an inexpensive, three-dimensional opportunity to share an experience of *you*.

9. Involve yourself in your community on an issue you are passionate about. In the giving you will receive.

10. Offer articles to local media and professional newsletters on what you're doing. Write about where your passion comes from. Share who you are and why you are devoting this stage of your life to this endeavor.

11. List yourself and your company in all appropriate directories . . . [S]eek out publications that specialize in your niche.

12. Let a long list of people know about your next gala author signing (lecture, or seminar). Ask twenty-five friends and colleagues to go through their Rolodex, to make calls to five of their friends.

13. Pitch a feature on you and your *unique* company to the local cable and newspaper features editor. Creatively present what is exceptional about your endeavor, and why it will make a difference in the world.

And last, but certainly not least, address your quality of life issues:

14. Make more of an investment in yourself. Ask: what assignments or activities can I streamline? What can I delegate? What can I eliminate altogether? What's the one thing I can let go of in order to take this company to the next level?

15. Learn to under-promise and over-deliver. Existing in a state of overwhelm doesn't serve us. Take on less and enjoy the thrill of an accomplishment thoroughly fulfilled.

16. Set higher standards for your own personal time every day. Take a half-hour walk—or take a nap—in the middle of the work day.

17. Stop tolerating. Make a list of twenty items you are procrastinating about and a second list of three goals you'd like to reach in the next ninety days.

18. To gain fresh perspective and a good rest, take twenty-four hours off four times a year. Go away by yourself on a soul retreat to a beautiful setting. Go fishing, for example. Personally, I don't fish but I hear it's the time between fish when we reconnect with our most peaceful inner selves.

(Excerpted from an article in SPAN Connection, *with permission of the author.)*

Maggie Klee Lichtenberg is a personal and business coach whose specialty is book publishing. A former publishing company executive (Simon & Schuster, Bantam, Grove Press, Beacon Press), Maggie was a featured speaker at the 1998 SPAN conference in Baltimore. If you are interested in individual or group coaching, call her at (505) 986-8807 or e-mail *margaretkl@aol.com.* "I offer a free half hour phone coaching session to support you in two issues that are draining your energy, and to target three reasonable ninety-day goals," she says.

Nonwriting Business

Just as a soldier becomes involved in a variety of nonmilitary activities—evacuations, humanitarian relief, national disasters, national security—so too does the guerrilla writer. The more you are involved in self-marketing, in fact, the more peripheral activities develop. Speaking engagements, teaching, and public appearances have become a mainstay for many scribes, often generating more income than their writing.

I first got involved in writing through a journalism course at the University of La Verne. Seven years later, I was teaching that course for the same school. As a student, I was like millions of others who dreamed of success and fame. I would someday be in the ranks of John Irving and Arthur Hailey if only I knew the right approach and the right format. In addition to this, it had sounded like an easy college credit. Fortunately, there is a never-ending flow of "wannabe writers" and, therefore, a constant need for professionals who can teach the skills and techniques of creative fiction, journalism, and freelance marketing.

If you are an active writer, perhaps the greatest advantage of teaching is that you get paid to talk about yourself. During my one-day seminars, I bring examples of my published work, discuss the step-by-step process of how each sale was made and go into the minute details of marketing. I never pretend that I can teach anyone to write—I cannot. I do, however, tell potential students that if they possess the ability to write, I can show them how to sell their work. This is because my expertise lies in writing and marketing nonfiction. I am, in a sense, a word "mechanic" rather than a creative writer.

In the early 1990s, I accompanied the popular country music group, Pirates of the Mississippi, on a tour through Germany, working as a marketing manager. During that time, the group began contemplating a song that would ultimately become the hit single called *I Think Locally.* That is exactly what you need to do—think locally, not create a hit single—if you want to break into the teaching field. If you have no experience, try contacting local libraries, social organizations like the YMCA/YWCA, or public schools. In most cases, you will be volunteering your services as a guest speaker. At the same time, however, you will be polishing your skills as a lecturer and, ultimately, a teacher. There are also organizations that can help you develop your ability to communicate with others face to face. Among these are the American Society for Training and Development *(www.astd.org),* Toastmasters International *(www.toastmasters.org),* and Langevin *(www.langevin.org).*

I expanded my writing career into the areas of speaking and teaching by first providing complimentary talks at a local library and middle school (grades 7–9). Through a friend I also lined up a discussion for a regional business association. This not only gave me confidence in speaking, it was a key factor in landing two corporate jobs. Armed with my newly acquired—albeit limited—speaking experience, I was ready to tell the world about my writing experiences and make money doing so. But where was I to begin?

Once again my media kit came into play. Before arbitrarily spending money on printing, photocopies, and postage, I sat down and came up with several target markets for what I was offering. Among these were colleges and universities, clubs and organizations, bookstores and businesses. I then researched each area, gathering college catalogs to see what was already offered, checking to see which private associations sponsored seminars, exploring which local high schools provided adult education classes, and making a list of bookstores that frequently hosted authors. For the business market, I was looking for medium-sized companies, without public relations departments, that could benefit from media exposure. This would allow me to offer a seminar on how to get free publicity through press releases. I found several of these companies.

The next step was to target my media kit to each market. I took on colleges and universities first, preparing a course outline for a two-day seminar on freelance writing. Based on the catalogs I'd collected, I was able to incorporate each school's classroom time requirement, and other aspects necessary for students to obtain credit for the course. This same basic outline was then used for clubs and organizations in a one-day format. I offered bookstores an even shorter version of the class (a mere four hours), to cover only query letters and the basic approach to nonfiction writing. Businesses, on the other hand, received a full-blown, one-week seminar proposal.

Once ready for delivery, I called each potential client and inquired to whom such proposals should be addressed. The following day UPS made the deliveries. Within a week, I had lined up the freelance writing course at the University of La Verne. Because I'd written several articles on archaeology, I was also asked to give a paid lecture at the International Archaeology Society, which met every month at a local church hall. Over the next year I would continue to teach classes for the college, as well as conduct adult education courses and run weekend seminars for the United Service Organization. My lecturing gigs during this same period expanded to include businesses, travel groups, and a variety of clubs and organizations.

Teaching Profits

Generally, colleges pay by the hour for semester-long courses. A seminar, on the other hand, will normally bring a flat fee. I've been offered from $10 to $30 per hour and $200 to $600 for one-day seminars. This wide range indicates that there are no real standards. What I like to do is investigate what is currently being paid to professors for seminars. Then, if I am happy with that, I go forward. If the rate seems too low, I'll offer a profit-sharing arrangement. In fact, with smaller organizations, adult education classes, and lectures, I frequently include this in my proposal. For example, if a two-day seminar is going to be priced at $75 a person, and I anticipate thirty students, this means the school or organization will take in $2,250. I might, therefore, offer the class for a fifty-fifty percentage of the profit. Naturally, if only ten students sign up, I lose out.

To increase student turnout, I do not depend on the marketing efforts of schools or organizations. I promote my own classes through press releases and kits to local media, college newspapers, and radio and television stations. For example, the first two-day seminar I taught for the University of La Verne was titled, "Write for Your Life." This was not an original name but one I borrowed from Art Spikol, a popular nonfiction writer and once columnist for *Writer's Digest*. The university anticipated thirty students. I had agreed to $35 a student, expecting to make just over $500 a day—minus time and money involved in preparing and sending out the press kits.

Two days after sending out the kits, I received a call from the local newspaper, the college magazine, and the university radio station. A week before the class, I was also asked to appear on a regionally broadcast television program to discuss my writing. I naturally took this opportunity to mention the seminar. The media coverage resulted in sixty-eight students, more than the local campus had ever had for a single seminar. My cut was $2,380—but I actually took home even more. You see, when negotiating the deal, I had arranged to provide all course materials—copies of sample query letters, manuscript formats, published articles, list of references. The college administrator had agreed that $5 would be charged for the package as part of the total course fee. This move brought me an additional $340.

Today I include my book, *The Writer's and Photographer's Guide to Global Markets*, as part of the "required reading," resulting in an additional $11 per student, after I've paid the publisher.

Where the big money lies, however, are classes or lectures to large corporations. You can charge from $250 to $3,000 a day to teach business people how to do their jobs better by using printed words. Or, if you have an expertise in a specific business sector, you can lecture on this topic. Corporations normally refer to such classes as "training." Perhaps this is because it makes attendees feel more like they are updating their professional skills rather than returning to school for a "class" or a "seminar." Here, too, you should try to produce and provide "training" materials yourself—and add it to the bill.

Expanding Your Niche

Once you get into the swing of teaching and/or lecturing, you might discover, as did I, that the same marketing techniques used to expand sales of your products can also be applied to increase profits in this sector of your business. With a slight twist of subject, for instance, you can go from teaching, say, freelance writing, to Journalism 101. Or you could introduce a creative writing course if that is where your talents lie.

Like any business venture, starting up is the most difficult part of teaching. Once you have achieved success in your specialty field, however, it becomes very easy to expand your services into other areas. I began with freelance writing (how to sell your words) because I was comfortable with the subject matter. During the past two decades I have broadened this to include: newspaper journalism, freelance photography, writing and selling nonfiction books, selling fiction, marketing your talents, and computer basics.

By expanding my teaching areas, I also developed a following of students—often seeing the same individuals enroll in my classes over and over again. It therefore became easy for me to estimate the number of students I would have and the amount of money I could expect from each class.

More and more writers today are finding fun and profit in speaking engagements. In his book, *Niche Marketing,* which is subtitled *How to Make Yourself Indispensable, Slightly Immortal, and Lifelong Rich in 18 Months,* author and publisher Gordon Burgett points out: "Talks and speeches sound the same to the outsider but there's a huge difference if you're giving them for a living: talks are free, speeches are paid!"

You should always keep this in mind, and strive to line up as many speeches as possible—though don't avoid "talking," particularly when it is about you and might generate additional work.

"I speak to service groups and community outreach programs often produced by hospitals in my city. Even though these are often 'gratis' presentations, I make some money selling books and, again, getting my name and face and program in front of people. Speaking to groups is the most effective and least expensive form of advertising."

—Karen O'Connor, professional writer

But what does it take to get speaking gigs? According to Charlotte Libov of the ASJA Speakers Services Committee, a good start is to alter your media kit into a "Speaker's Kit."

The Speaker's Kit—*by Charlotte Libov* ©

As a writer, you may have gotten your first speaking engagement because someone just happened to see your byline on a book or a magazine article. And perhaps a few more bookings have come your way that way. But if you want to do more than an occasional presentation, you'll need to do more than passively wait for calls to come along. You need to take an active approach; you need to market yourself.

Many speakers find their first helpful step is to put together what I simply refer to as my "speaker's kit." It's very similar to the media kit I use to promote myself and my books to broadcast media. In fact, most of the components are identical. My media kit includes:

- a pitch letter to the producer of the radio or TV show, focusing on specific topics based on my book;

- a news release about the book;
- biographical information about me;
- laudatory reviews and other clips about my book;
- pertinent articles I've written;
- a photograph of myself and/or the book jacket.

My speaker's kit includes all of the above. The pitch letter is of course directed to an organization officer, meeting planner, or other appropriate individual, and the letter is broader in scope, citing a number of topics I can address. And there are two important additions that turn my media kit into a speaker's kit: my one-sheet and a sheaf of testimonials.

A *one-sheet* is a single 8½-by-11–inch sheet of paper covering the same kind of information you would include in a brochure: a head shot and at least one photo showing you in action as a speaker; your speaking topics; your credentials; persuasive copy touting your prowess as a speaker (including a succinct philosophy or mission statement if you have one); a list of clients, with five or six quotes from satisfied users of your speaking services (obviously not possible if you're just starting out); information on how to get in touch with you. (If you work strictly through a lecture bureau or agency, you would omit the contact information, leaving space for the agency to furnish its own contact information.)

The brochure or one-sheet is the key element in your speaker's kit and must be able to stand alone, as well; it's what you'll put in the mail, or fax, to an individual who expressly requests a single piece of literature. Whether to use a brochure or a one-sheet is up to you. I happen to prefer the latter; to view my own one-sheet, visit *www.libov.com/speaking.html.*

Testimonials, known more formally as letters of recommendation, are so important that you shouldn't sit back and wait for them to arrive unsolicited. Never hesitate to speak up. Starting with your very first talk, even if it's an unpaid presentation to the PTA, ask for a letter of recommendation or, better still, send a written request. I generally include that request in a letter thanking the meeting planner for having me and saying how much I enjoyed the experience.

My request for a recommendation is straightforward and explicit. I suggest that the letter include such information as the size of the audience (if it was a large crowd), the topic I covered, and a selection of favorable comments received. You may not feel comfortable asking for such a letter at first (I certainly didn't), but this is too useful a tool to neglect. These letters and the quotes they contain can be extremely valuable in your marketing endeavors.

All of the items I've listed will fit comfortably in the two-pocket folder generally used for press kits. And don't forget to include a business card.

As you grow in your speaking career, and begin vying for higher fees, you may want to consider having an audio- and/or videotape made of your presentations; these tapes can be sent to prospective clients. To be effective, however, they must be done professionally, and that can run to hundreds of dollars; this particular promotional tool may have to wait.

Speakers vary in how they use these tools. I generally mail or fax my one-sheet along with any other promotional effort (such as a news release on a new book), as well as give them out whenever I meet someone who casually mentions that he or she books speakers—or knows someone who books speakers. I reserve the full speaker's kit for sending to those who specifically request information on my speaking services. You'll get a feeling for what works for you.

Good guidance on constructing a speaker's kit, as well as lots of additional information about professional speaking, may be found in Mike Frank's book, *For Professional Speakers Only.*

(reprinted from ASJA Newsletter,
with permission from the author and ASJA)

If you are looking for a way to jump-start your speaking career, here are a couple of other tips:

- Get involved in the National Speakers Association. You can find information on this group at its Web site: *www.nsa.speaker.org.*
- Sign up for the free Internet newsletter *SpeakerNet.* This provides a wealth of tips and information on this moneymaking business. You should send an e-mail to Rebecca Morgan *(rlmorgan@aol.com)* to get on the mailing list.

Public Appearances

Author, speaker, and consultant Jan Larkey is one of the most successful marketers in the business. She regularly appears on television and other media. In every case, there is a long-term goal—and you can learn from her example.

"I appeared on QVC as an expert, then continued as an author. I gave audiences tips on why they should buy style X—how it would enhance their hips, waist, height, etc. My first appearance was as a result of being referred by a friend/owner of a full-figured modeling agency in New York who promoted large-size clothing on another channel that was bought by QVC."

After writing *Flatter Your Figure,* released by Simon & Schuster's Fireside imprint as a paperback book selling for $10, Larkey returned to QVC. She was still an expert, but this time she not only gave advice, she sold her book.

"We sold 10,000 copies in that one day! It was the first book sold (1991) and really got the attention of publishers," Jan explains. "Later orders were in the 5,000-book range. In total, we sold over 40,000 copies."

Jan offers the following advice to writers seeking to enhance their book sales, or achieve visibility as experts through television and/or personal appearances:

- Learn to deliver a dynamite message from the plat-form. You will get paid for performances that pro-mote your books (products, or self). Join local speaking associations. For beginners: Toastmasters or the National Speaker's Association.
- Take media training. Five-minute TV segments are over before you blink! Learn to use sound bites and get your message across quickly and professionally. Al Parinello (Tel: (201) 784-0059) will train you via five phone lessons.
- Advertise your topic/expertise in *Radio-TV Interview Report* to get booked on local, regional, and nation-al shows (Tel: (800) 989-1400).
- In TV studios, give out a short statement about how people can get your book (or service or product) to the phone operator—for any call-in inquiries—plus the producer and your host. Ask for this informa-tion to be put on the screen.
- Take a blank ¾-inch videotape to the TV station. Ask for a dub of your segment. Use it to create a demo tape to get on other shows and gain speaking engagements.

INTERNET MARKETING

You and I live in exciting times. Technology has gone from manual to electronic typewriters, to computers with word processing programs, to the Internet. I cannot imagine any successful writer today not utilizing the so-called information superhighway, since it takes your marketing ability to new heights. The Internet has revolutionized the way writers do business. Global markets are suddenly at your fingertips. Opportunities abound—both for self-promotion and sales potential. It will not be long before all editors, all over the world, are working through e-mail, and rightly so. It eases their workload—articles and even books can be sent in formats that require no retyping—and allows them to work with a far wider range of professionals around the world.

"As I write a great deal about the Net, I put some effort into maintaining my Web pages. I link to as much of my work on the Web as I can find, and strongly encourage anyone publishing my work on the Web to link back to my page, so that readers who are interested can click through and get information about my book and other activities."

—*Wendy M. Grossman, American author in London*

Your Web Site

Every writer should have a Web page, if for no other reason than to provide a résumé of his professional credits. Most Internet Service Providers (ISP), because of tough competition, have begun offering free Internet Web pages as part of an annual subscription. My server, for example, gives me up to one megabyte of space for Web pages as well as two e-mail boxes.

I could have gone to a professional site designer for my page—many people do. But I found the step-by-step process for creating my own Web site in Microsoft Publisher so easy that I decided to do it on my own. You can take a look at the results at *www.cybernet.it/sedge*. My goal was to list credits, highlight my books, and provide testimonials from past clients—in addition to listing contact information.

If you are new to the Web game, or have never gotten around to creating your own site, you can get a quick course in using HTML (Internet format) at these sites:

- A Beginner's Guide to HTML
  www.ncsa.uiuc.edu/General/Internet/WWW/HTMLPrimerP1.html
- Introduction to HTML
  www.cwru.edu/help/introHTML/toc.html

- Netscape Enhancement Guide
  www.ibic.com/Program/NscapeHome.html

Armed with a Web page, I am able to direct editors and other potential clients there to review my credits. This, I believe, is the greatest advantage to an Internet site. This type of marketing, however, only works if customers know that your page exists. For this, you must promote the site.

One of the easiest ways to get people to visit your Internet site is by exchanging banners, or tiny ads, with owners of other Web pages. A year ago I exchanged banners with a freelance photographer. Because his work sold to hundreds of magazines and newspapers around the world, many editors who reviewed his pages were then drawn to mine. After all, it merely required them to click on the little box at the bottom of the photographer's Web site that read: "Don't Think You Can Afford a *Newsweek* Writer? Click here to find out."

I specifically chose this wording—after selling my last article to *Newsweek*—to stimulate curiosity, and it worked! Several assignments have come in as a result of this banner, and I still get inquiries through it. My next step was simply to expand my Web marketing, to increase the number of cooperative banner deals I could make, and to get my site listed in as many places as possible. The more you are seen—in print, in public, on the Web—the more traffic you can direct to your page, and the more work you will receive.

You should include your Web site address, whenever possible, in any published work. Each month I write features for several publications—some on the Internet, others in print media. In every case I request that the editor run a blurb about my professional work and include my Web site address. Anyone wishing to know more about me can therefore review this electronic "billboard." Three months ago, in fact, I received an e-mail from an editor in Los Angeles.

During a trip to Asia, he'd read one of my articles in *Silver Kris,* the in-flight magazine of Singapore Airlines. Upon his return to the United States, he'd looked at my Web site—listed at the bottom of the article—where he obtained my electronic mail address. In his message he pointed out that he'd enjoyed the *Silver Kris* feature and wondered if first North American serial rights were available.

Piggyback Marketing

In addition to creating and promoting your own Web page, you should try to get Internet publishers with whom you work to market your services on their sites, whenever possible. Authorlink.com, for instance, has a section that highlights the writers who work for it, as do Tropi-ties.com and many others. Be sure to inquire about this when selling to Internet magazines. If you find out that the publication offers author listings, request to be included. Then provide the editor with as much information as possible, including a photo. I began taking advantage of these opportunities three years ago. As a result, I currently have over twenty-seven Web sites where potential clients can find my personal and professional information. I am included on my agent's Web site, as well as those of Articles International, a syndication operation in Canada for whom I work, and numerous publications.

When *The Writer's and Photographer's Guide to Global Markets* was published, I arranged cooperative sales agreements with Internet publishers such as *Writer On Line* and *Authorlink.* I then offered my services as a columnist to *Writer On Line.* Because *Writer On Line* was a relatively new operation, I realized that the pay would not be outstanding. So I contemplated how I could assist *Writer On Line* and, in turn, how the site could assist me. The answer, to which the publisher quickly agreed, was Web space and exposure. I would write a monthly column on international marketing; in exchange, I would receive a small payment, a link (a highlighted area that readers can click on to automatically go to a new page) to my personal Web site, a Web page for the sale of my book, and a banner on the cover of the magazine each month that, when clicked, linked to the book sale page.

After writing the column for five months, I also proposed an online writing course to the publisher. The proposal called for *Writer On Line* to market the class and handle registration. In exchange, *Writer On Line* would receive a percentage of the profits. As a result, two new Web pages were developed. But it did not stop there. *Writer On Line* also blitzed readers with my book and course in its bimonthly promotional newsletter:

> This is the first issue of *Writer On Line* for 1999. In the coming year, look for a much-expanded Marketplace department and a brand new look from our graphics department, as well as other features including our first online course from marketing guru Mike Sedge. We enjoyed serving you in 1998 and look forward to creating an even richer experience in the coming months. We wish our 20,000 subscribers a happy and prosperous New Year.
>
> Price Change: The price for our new CD, "Software Dreampack for Writers," will increase on February 1. Dreampack is a collection of 57 writers' programs—virtually all the writing software the Internet has to offer—on one CD. Details at *www.novalearn.com/dp*. Limited Offer: Buy the Writer's Software Companion and get a free copy of Software Dreampack for Writers, while supplies last.
>
> New Online Course from Michael Sedge—"Going Global with Your Writing Career." Learn the skills and techniques of selling your articles again and again throughout the world, with veteran marketer Michael Sedge. For information: *www.novalearn.com/writers/ sedge/sedgecourse.htm*.

NEW THIS ISSUE

www.novalearn.com/wol

—Nancy Kress answers more readers' questions in "What to Write and When to Write It."

—In "Plot Is a Four-Letter Word," writer Alex Keegan argues that attention to theme and character drives a better story and allows a richer, more satisfying plot to evolve rather than be imposed.

—Mike Sedge reveals insights about international rights.

—Playwrights, a modest proposal from Linda Eisenstein: If you're serious about learning to write for the stage, you need to turn off your TV right now!

—Do you have to write every day? Peggy Tibbetts answers this and more in "The Truth About Being a Writer."

—A new Writer's Crossword Puzzle by Nelson Hardy

—"Hamlet's Soliloquy for Writers," a new Web Lite

—New listings in Conferences, Contests and Marketplace

AND 14 continuing articles . . .

$$$$$$ HELP WANTED $$$$$$$

The Writer's Software Companion offers an extremely simple Associates Program from which you can earn considerable income with little effort. For details, send the one-word message "career" to *career@novalearn.com*. An autoresponder will send you details by e-mail. Mail to: *career@novalearn.com*.

WRITING TEACHERS: If you are a teacher of writing in a college, university, or community workshop setting, you can make generous commissions selling The Writer's Software Companion at volume discounts. For information see *www.novalearn.com/writers/teachers.htm*

Writer On Line is a paying market. We are looking for timely, professionally written articles that offer keen insight and solid advice on the craft and marketing of writing of all kinds. For details, send an e-mail with the content "writers" to *writers@novalearn.com*. Information will be sent by autoresponder. Mail to: *writers@ novalearn.com*.

Writer On Line is still recruiting Associate Editors in certain areas. These are not salaried positions but do offer financial considerations. For details, send an e-mail with the content "editors" to *editors@novalearn.com*. Information will be sent by autoresponder. Mail to: *editors@novalearn.com*.

PRODUCTS AND SERVICES

Learn the secrets of going global with your freelance work and how to double your income through global sales. MIKE SEDGE offers a complete approach to selling articles and photographs abroad, including more than one thousand e-mail addresses around the world. Chapters cover agents, editors, art directors, publishers, and stock houses overseas. *www.novalearn.com/writers/ sedge/sedge.htm*.

ADVERTISE! Put your classified ads here. Now over 20,000 subscribers mailed twice a month. Ad repeated on Web site. For ad-rate card, go to *www.novalearn. com/rates.htm*.

TO UNSUBSCRIBE
To unsubscribe from this list just e-mail: *list@novalearn.com*
Message: unsubscribe

SOFTWARE DREAMPACK FOR WRITERS
www.novalearn.com/dp
THE WRITER'S SOFTWARE COMPANION
www.novalearn.com

WORDWRIGHT Critique Service *www.novalearn.com/ww*
THE WRITER'S INTERNET RESOURCE GUIDE
www.novalearn.com/wirg

Writer On Line © 1999 Novation Learning Systems, Inc.
(Reprinted with permission of the publisher)

Within twenty-four hours of sending out this information, *Writer On Line* received three sign-ups for the class. I, on the other hand, received an offer from another Internet publisher to run a similar writing class through its Web site. So, as you can see, it pays to work with Internet publishers to enhance your exposure. If you can arrange a banner as part of your payment for articles, take it. If you can list your Web site, e-mail address, or both, at the end of articles, do so. And if a publisher is in a position to offer you a free Web page, ask for it. The key is to consistently think marketing when working over the Internet.

Most people fail to understand that their Web site will not necessarily be part of the global search systems. That is, when an editor is looking for "writers" using AltaVista, Yahoo!, HotBot, Mamma, or one of the other popular Internet search engines, your name and Web page may not appear. This is because you are not registered with these companies. There are several ways that you can submit your page to major search engines. Start by asking your ISP; the ISP may be able to do this for you. Another option is to submit your name to *www.execpc.com/~mbr/bookwatch/writepub/#pubsearch*. While this is normally used for publishers, you can include yourself as a provider of editorial services.

The secret to successfully marketing yourself, your services, and your products over the information superhighway boils down to exposure. The more you can get your site listed with search engines and in directories, announcements, Web magazines, mailing lists, Web news services, and newsgroups, the more traffic you will have and, as a result, the greater your business.

Using a Signature

One of the easiest promotional tools to take advantage of is the signature feature offered by contemporary e-mail programs. If you don't already use one, you have no doubt seen them on incoming messages. For instance, my own signature currently looks like this:

Michael Sedge
STRAWBERRY MEDIA
Via Venezia 14/b
80021 Afragola (NA) Italy
Tel: (011) 39-081-851-2208
Fax: (011) 39-081-851-2210
E-mail: *pp10013@cybernet.it*

www.cybernet.it/sedge
www.novelearn.com/wol/archeives/archives.htm#mike
www.novelearn.com/writers/sedge/sedge.htm
www.novelearn.com/writers/sedge/sedgecourse.htm

Each of the Web pages listed below my e-mail address will link potential customers to a page containing information about myself and my services. The *www.cybernet.it/sedge* site provides my general résumé, while *www.novelearn.com/wol/archives/archives/htm@mike* connects to a listing of past columns for *Writer On Line.*

Like a gun without bullets, a signature is a useless marketing tool unless properly maintained. Each month you should update your listings, ensuring that all links are current and accurate. If you've recently published a feature on the Internet, include it. At the same time, weed out any old listings.

Maintaining a good signature does not take long. It can, however, enhance your sales. After I began including a signature with Internet links, the requests for clips and information on my professional activities stopped coming in. Editors with Internet capabilities simply clicked on the links I provided and found more than enough information to know if I was right for a particular job.

"Get noticed on newsgroups. You don't sell much writing that way, but it generates lasting impressions. Also, try to develop a 'signature' book with which people identify you, whether you make money off that book or not."

—*Skip Press, author of Writer's Guide to Hollywood Producers, Directors, and Screenwriter's Agents*

Be a Groupie

Usenet newsgroups are an excellent way to create a network of colleagues as well as find work. Additionally, being a regular participant in various online groups will get your name in the various marketplaces. Despite what some writers think, it is my experience that numerous agents, editors, and publishers spend time reading and discussing various aspects of their business in these virtual conference rooms.

Two years ago, for instance, a discussion of horror came up in the newsgroup alt.writing. Having recently completed a novel in this genre, I began reading what others had to say. One writer suggested that, due to the difficulty unknown novelists have in selling work of this type, they might consider entering unpublished novels in international competitions. I took his advice and, ultimately, won an award for my work in the United Kingdom. I announced this to the group last year and included the contest Web site, which ran an excerpt of my unpublished book. The following day I received a letter from a New York agent saying:

> Dear Mr. Sedge,
> I read the sample of your award-winning novel on the NovelAdvice Web site and am impressed with your style and storyline. If you do not already have an agent for this work, I would be happy to consider it. A hard copy of the completed book should be sent to my office for final consideration.

This agent is now representing my novel, soliciting publishers in the Big Apple as well as London.

No matter what your interest, there is a newsgroup that covers it, or so it seems. A quick Internet search under the journalism classification reveals, for example, that there are such groups as freelance, gay-press, music, newspapers, photography, print media, students, and others. Under the writers category, you can join discussions among songwriters, tech writers, screenwriters, poets, and even unemployed writers.

If you discover that a classification for your interest does not exist—say, writers specializing in underwater pineapple production—you can create your own discussion group at Yahoo.com. The Yahoo Clubs at *http://clubs.yahoo.com* allow you to establish Internet groups covering a variety of topics. Among the general classifications already created are: Business & Finance, Computers & Internet, Cultures & Communities, Entertainment & Art, Books, Games, Recreation & Sports, Religion & Beliefs, Science, Sex & Romance.

Any group you create, as well as those already established, can be used to send people to your Web site. When you post a message, for instance, always include your Web site address under your name. Or, if you are specifically pointing out something about yourself or your work, you might say "Take a look at my Web site for examples." Then provide the Web address. Newsgroups can also be used as networking tools to generate business for you and others. Here is an example of how it might work:

> Jim—"I specialize in interviews. I was offered a free-lance job in London last week, but had to turn it down. The cost of the trip would have been more than the editor wanted to pay."

> You—"Hi, Jim. I plan to be in London next month, do you think the editor is still looking for someone?"

> Jim—"Could be. Send an e-mail to Todd Mann at *toddm@editor.com*. Tell him I sent you."

> You—Thanks. By the way, if you have any interviews of political figures, you might be able to sell U.K. rights to *Ambassador* magazine. The editor there is Mark McWilliams at *mc@ambassador.com*.

Engaging in open discussion and sharing information—that's what newsgroups are all about. How effectively you use these will depend a great deal on your willingness to participate and offer information. Over the past year, I have obtained editorial jobs based on input from writers in California, New York, Dallas, Ontario, Bali, Paris, and London. At the same time, I have provided leads that have led to several published articles and at least one book. It's a big world out there, with hundreds of thousands of opportunities. Don't be afraid to offer contacts to colleagues. It will come back to you ten times over, believe me.

Seeking Employment on the Net

I have been self-employed for twenty years. I have no desire to ever work as an employee again. The thought of a nine-to-five job, requiring me to punch a time card, produce on demand, and report to a "boss" holds no interest. Then why, you might ask, does my name appear on several Internet job sites, wherein I am seeking employment?

Ten years ago, when I had my own employees, I realized that each dependent cost much—MUCH—more than their weekly paycheck indicated. For example, if your gross salary was $40,000 a year, in reality you would cost me $54,000 after adding hospitalization, insurance, taxes, and so on. It therefore occurred to me that publishers and corporate managers—particularly those heading startup magazines or those who merely need an in-house writer—would be far better off hiring me as an independent contractor to do their work than to get tied to an employee. Convincing these individuals that my offer was a better deal than a nine-to-five worker was my challenge—and should be yours.

Joel Jacobs, a good friend and colleague, edited the Italian magazine the *World of Beer* from his office in Dallas for many years, even though the publisher was in Milan. Similarly, *R&R Magazine*'s editor, Marjorie Hess, lives in Chicago. The publication, however, is put together, printed, and distributed from the company headquarters in Germany. The point is that contemporary technology allows anyone to be an editor without having to be physically on site.

Using my insight into these two aspects of editorial positions—(1) that employees cost about 35 percent more than contracted workers and (2) that I could easily edit a publication from my base in Italy—I set out to get jobs that allowed me to work "my way."

My first four tries—two corporate writer positions, a senior editor job, and one slot as an assistant editor—fell flat. This was primarily because I was dealing with a personnel manager rather than directly with an editor-in-chief or publisher who understood the value of what I was offering. Next, I received a call from an executive from the World Wildlife

Fund's Mediterranean Headquarters in Rome. He invited me
to an interview to "discuss my unique proposal." The meeting—three executives and myself—went well. Alas, the deal
fell through when they offered two-thirds less than I wanted.

Ultimately, however, I convinced two publications
that what they really needed was not an office staff writer,
but a contract writer. This resulted in a combined fee
($1,200) to produce three articles a month—each less than
400 words. Eventually, additional work came from both
magazines, which increased my overall annual revenue.

When companies advertise for an editor or staff
writer, they have a need to fill. In most cases, an executive
or publisher makes the decision about who to hire. These
executives rarely, if ever, explore an alternative solution. It
is therefore your job to present them with the alternative—
you—and sell them on the professionalism, quality, and reliability you offer. I do this through my credits, high-caliber
references, and clips (see Creating Your Kit in chapter 7).

Two weeks ago, for example, I received an employment announcement by e-mail from Jeff Leach, editor-in-
chief of *Discovering Archaeology*. Because the developments
surrounding this position perfectly illustrate how you can
utilize full-time job openings to gain freelance work, I'd like
to share the correspondence with you.

Senior Editor
Position Available Immediately

DISCOVERING ARCHAEOLOGY MAGAZINE
Must have strong writing and editorial skills applica-
ble to a mixed lay and professional readership.

Working closely with the Editor-in-Chief, Managing Editor, and Senior Science Editor, the Senior
Editor will be responsible for overseeing in-house
writers, working with outside writers, interacting

with art department, and writing for the magazine. Background in archaeology a plus.

If you have these qualifications please send your résumé and samples of your writing immediately to: Editor-in-Chief *(jleach@elp.rr.com)*. Discovering Archaeology Magazine, 1205 N. Oregon, El Paso, Texas 79902, USA. Tel: (915) 533-8503; Fax: (915) 544-9276. Please include salary history. We offer excellent benefits, and salary is negotiable.

To: Jeff Leach / Discovering Archaeology Magazine
From: Michael Sedge / Strawberry Media Agency
Subject: Senior Editor

Dear Jeff,
Thanks for sending information on the Senior Editor position.

Having recently worked for Earthwatch and the Discovery Channel, as well as having a history of archaeological topics among my 2,500 articles and seven books, the job is of interest to me.

I was contracted in June as the on-site writer for the Discovery Channel's book and documentary project, *Cleopatra,* in Alexandria, Egypt. I spent weeks with French archaeologist and researcher Frank Goddio exploring the underwater finds of the ancient city of the Ptolemaïs. The documentary and book will be released in March.

This research also resulted in my writing features on this topic for Mobil Oil's *Compass* and Singapore Airlines' *Silver Kris* magazines.

My writings have included several Earthwatch projects over the past fifteen years, including digs at Pompeii, Italy and areas of Switzerland and the United States. Most recently, I did a general piece on joining an archaeological dig, which sold to Philippine Airlines' *Mabuhay, R&R Magazine* (Germany), *Tropi-Ties* (U.S.-Internet), and *Informer* (Italy).

Based in Europe, I additionally covered archaeology extensively for The Associated Press and Time-Life Books between 1980 and 1990.

My books, *Commercialization of the Oceans* and *The Adventure Guide to Italy,* also delve into the world of archaeology, both above and below the water's surface—i.e., the sunken Roman City of Baiae, Italian digs, etc.

The fact that I live in Europe (getting to the United States four or five times a year), and work closely with a number of research and archaeology groups, brings added advantage to you. I would offer the following benefits:

• Expanded coverage—Europe and Middle East—for *Discovering Archaeology* magazine.

• An on-site writer for breaking news—new finds in Pompeii (which is in my backyard).

• Rather than an employee, I am willing to work as a contractor—thus reducing the cost of benefits, social security, etc.

• As I am a long-time member of the American Society of Journalists and Authors (recently nominated president of the European chapter, though we still need to vote), you are ensured high quality and professionalism.

• Because I speak fluent English, Italian, and some French and Spanish, doors are more easily opened to me.

• Writing archaeology for the layman has been a trademark of mine for several years.

• Modern technology would allow weekly and daily contact with *Discovering Archaeology* editors for immediate needs. One of the aspects of my business that has pleased editors around the world is my ability to write on demand. This is a technique acquired through years of news writing. I am able to write and research any topic and turn out a comprehensive story under tight deadline.

Given the above, I would anticipate two trips to the U.S. office a year to attend editorial/planning meetings. Beyond this, work would be conducted from the "Discovery Archaeology European Office" and sent by e-mail/courier each month.

Below I am enclosing a recent biography, and will be happy to provide clips. If you'd like to check references, here are a couple of people you could contact:

John Buffalo, the Discovery Channel, *John_Buffalo @discovery.com*

Blue Magruder, Earthwatch, *bmagruder@earth-watch.org*

Marjorie Hess, *R&R Magazine, rrcom@ameritech.net*

I look forward to hearing from you and hope we can work together.

Sincerely,

Michael Sedge
Strawberry Media
Via Venezia 14/b
80021 Afragola (NA) Italy
Tel: (011) 39-081-851-2208
Fax: (011) 39-081-851-2210
Toll free: (800) 340-7713
E-mail: *pp10013@cybernet.it*
Web: *www.cybernet.it/sedge*

Michael:
Thanks for your lengthy message. Based on the information you provided, a good fit looks possible. However, we are looking for someone to work in-house. Nevertheless, I would like to figure out how we can work together. A little about who we are: I started the magazine in June of this year and the first issue (bimonthly) will be on the stand in late December. We do have a European Editor . . . [who] provides us with a complete (edited, images, copy-

right stuff, etc.) "European" article for each magazine . . . We get researchers to write most stories but . . . this has a drawback in that most of the articles require heavy editing. Most of the scientists write for their colleagues and not for a lay public. As it stands now, we rework the material with a small staff—however, with any new startup magazine, we are shorthanded and everyone is working on hundreds of things at once. This is where the Senior Editor(s) come in—and we need professional help.

As for you and I—how can we make this work?

1. Do you want to contribute the occasional (one or so an issue) short piece (the latest and greatest from your part of the world)

2. write longer pieces for each issue

3. edit and clean up material I send you from El Paso

4. or a combination of all three?

You also point out a problem I will face [with staff editors], the bucks. Just starting off, cash is a problem. This should get better by the second and third year. We are also planning an International version of the magazine for the second year as well as a German version.

So how can you and I work together (the communication is easy—e-mail solves those problems)? Do we put you on a monthly stipend and you agree to do this and that—or do we work on a piece basis? And the big question, how do I get you to work for less than you should get, with the agreement and hope that the magazine will grow and everyone's compensation with it?

Hope to talk to you soon.

Jeff D. Leach
Publisher and Editor-in-Chief
Discovering Archaeology Magazine
1205 North Oregon Street
El Paso, Texas 79902 U.S.A.
Tel: (915) 533-8503
Fax: (915) 544-9276
E-mail: *jleach@elp.rr.com*
Web: *www.discoveringarchaeology.com*

As I write this, Jeff and I are closing in on a deal that will have me producing a package for each issue. I will also be listed as the Mediterranean/Middle East Editor on both the print and electronic versions of the magazine. The monthly compensation will result in a per word rate of approximately $1 per word. Not bad for a job that will require, perhaps, ten days of work a month. And best of all, I can work in my PJs.

Radio/TV Promotion on the Internet— for a Fee

A relatively new business has sprung up as a result of the popularity of the Internet—showcasing writers on television and radio. While some people shun this type of marketing, others rave about it. One of the companies currently enjoying fair success—not only in obtaining customers, but in getting them bookings—is ShowIdeas.Com, subtitled "The Online Magazine for Guest and Show Ideas."

Very simply, ShowIdeas.Com creates a marketing site for you within its online archives. The listing contains your name, address, phone number, fax number, e-mail address, your guest availability information and, if appropriate, a copy of your book, or specialty, and press kit material. Oh yes, there is a fee of $125 per listing.

"Then just sit back and wait for your listing to appear and for journalists to call," explains ShowIdea.Com's instructions to potential clients. "We generally will put new listings on the site within two weeks or less of receiving the required materials."

Each listing is maintained for a minimum of twelve months. The site is operated by Susannah Greenberg Public Relations, 2166 Broadway, Suite 9E, New York, NY 10024. For more information, contact Robert Schechter by e-mail *(bob@bookbuzz.com)* or visit the ShowIdea.Com Web site.

If you're seeking radio gigs, try *www.RadioTour.com*. Operated by Broadcast Interview Source, the company reaches out to radio producers and talk show hosts across the country. As their promotion says, "Show the news media you're available. With RadioTour.com, we do all the work— and YOU do all the interviews."

There is a $295 fee for this service. For this you get: Web page space on a site frequented by print and broadcast media; your RealAudio® message included on your Radio Tour Web page; a press fax, including your interview availability, transmitted to a thousand media outlets; a press e-mail sent to ten thousand shows and journalists; and guaranteed exposure—or your listing will be run again for free.

For more information, visit the Radio Tour Web site or call (202) 333-4904.

A third company offering Internet promotional assistance is KeynotePage *(www.KeynotePage.com)*. "KeynotePage is a full-featured talking Web page that links to and drives business to your main Web site," explains company ads. "Or, use KeynotePage to establish your presence on the web."

Included in the KeynotePage package are: your voice in RealAudio®—a five-minute demo you can record on the phone; contact information; your photo; a book, if available; your text; your topics; and a link to your Web pages. In addition, your page will be indexed in the YearbookNews.com search engine. This was created for journalists seeking interview contacts and received up to a quarter of a million hits each month.

The fee is $195 per year. To receive greater detail, visit the KeynotePage Web site or call (800) KEYNOTE.

Packaging and Distribution

Packaging and distribution are two primary aspects of any marketing campaign. Each year, companies like Coca-Cola, Proctor & Gamble, and Ford spend millions of dollars to package and distribute products in a way that will enhance sales. The marketing staffs at these companies realize the importance of appearance and timely delivery, and so should you.

The method in which your work is submitted and presented will have a direct impact on the buyer's emotional state—positive or negative—as she considers your material. It is my belief—and that of millions of successful business people—that you should use everything in your power to ensure that a buyer's initial reaction to your product is positive. Whatever you are trying to sell—an article, a book, your services as a corporate writer or lecturer—you should always strive to make your product stand out from the crowd, make it unique. I have, for example, invested a great deal of time as well as a few dollars in my stationery. While this may seem like a simple matter, I feel that good stationery will help make sales—or at least gain assignments. This is particularly true if it presents a professional, "big company" image.

I had three goals in designing my stationery: (1) to promote all the products and services I offered, (2) to create a standard logo for each area of my business, (3) to make my company—and, by extension, myself—sound larger than life. In achieving these goals, I also succeeded in making the Strawberry Media stationery a marketing tool. Rather than take a standard approach, with the company address at the top, I ran a 1.75 × 11–inch box along the left side of the paper. This was then divided into six even-sized boxes. The first box contained the company logo, Strawberry Media, in red. Under this was "promotions" in blue. Next came a box with the same red logo, but under it, in yellow, was the word "communications." After this appeared the "editorial" (in black) and the "photo" (in green) boxes. Different typeface was used for each of the words below the company design.

These four distinct logos, while carrying the business name, each pointed out various aspects of my operation. They told editors that I am not a typical freelance writer. Rather, I am involved in a full-range of promotional, communications, editorial, and photographic activities.

The Big Image

I did not stop there, however. In the last two boxes I listed the address, phone and fax numbers, and e-mail addresses for both my North American and my European offices.

"When I noticed you had offices on both sides of the world," one editor told me, "I was immediately impressed."

If the truth were known, anyone visiting my Shelbyville, Tennessee, office, would find my father sitting at a computer passing e-mails, opening business letters, and performing other administrative functions for me. The European headquarters, on the other hand, is a one-room office that I have established in my home. This does not, however, make the Strawberry Media operation any less efficient than an editorial or stock photo service based in New York City.

If you are located in New York and have a relative or trusted friend in, say, Los Angeles, you could easily promote yourself as a multioffice operation. I am currently exploring a third office address—this time near Dallas—from which a friend will forward any business inquiries. The key is to present a large, corporate image.

My quest for impressive packaging goes beyond the letterhead. The Strawberry Media logo themes were carried over to my envelopes and business cards. I then had four-color presentation folders designed, featuring the four different business logos. Whether I am submitting a book proposal, a completed article, or some other project to a potential client, it is delivered in one of these folders. Upon opening it, he finds the matching business card and cover letter.

As with any business, operating a professional writing service requires an investment of both time and money. Don't be stingy when it comes to your packaging. At the same time, though, be sure you maximize the design, making it both informative and a sales tool. My own stationery and presentation folders offer a professional look; at the same time, the multiservice design has generated a good deal of crossover work. In 1994, for example, I was writing press releases for a major company when, from my stationery, a sales manager noticed that I also work in the promotional field. This resulted in a job coordinating a direct marketing campaign. In turn, this developed into an annual contract that included advertising design as well.

Another example occurred just last week with Earthwatch Institute. I had been trying to sell a story to Mark Cherrington, editor of *Earthwatch* magazine. While my efforts were unsuccessful, I did receive a call from Elizabeth Brown in the publications department. She needed images for their new catalog. This resulted in the sale of two photographs for $265.

Offering a Complete Package

Recently, an editor called me with an urgent need. He offered me only two days in which to research, write, and deliver a feature with photography. To make things worse, while the magazine was produced by a high-tech printing operation, the editor was not connected to the Internet or e-mail. I accepted the challenge just the same.

Completing the assignment in one day, I packaged it in my traditional style and called UPS; twenty-four hours later, it was sitting on the editor's desk. That evening he called to say, "You can accredit this sale to your superb packaging. The art director and printers love working with you."

What made my packaging—rather than writing—so unique that it would clinch this sale? Why was the art department and production staff so impressed?

In my package, I provided a hard copy of the article; a color-printed copy of the photographs and graphics (maps); a CD containing the digital images and graphics, with captions included; and the article in two standard word-processing formats (DOC and TXT). All of this went into a clear plastic envelope which, in turn, was placed into a Strawberry Media presentation folder. A cover letter was also included. I then completed the package with a business card—which fits into a slot inside the folder.

In the not too distant future, all editorial materials—text, graphics, and images—will be submitted electronically. Until that time comes, writers like you must know the capabilities—and limitations—of each editor you work with. It is safe to assume that all editors today work with computers. Not all of them, however, accept digital images. Additionally, any editor you work with will want you to provide text in a software format that is compatible with her own computer system.

The most common word processing programs used by writers and editors are WordPerfect and Microsoft Word. Contemporary versions of these and other word processing programs will, in most cases, convert files from one of the above formats to the other. Where you will most likely run into problems is when you are working with a new version of, say, Microsoft Word, and the editor is still using an older version. Microsoft Word 7.0, for example, can read the files of all earlier versions, but Microsoft Word 6.0 cannot read documents created on later-edition software.

Other problems of compatibility include loss of **bold**, *italics*, and <u>underlining</u>. In some cases, special characteristics as well as formatting come out as boxes, page breaks, or unrecognizable symbols. To overcome compatibility problems, always ask editors what formats their equipment can read. Then provide the completed text in that format, if possible. I recommend including a copy of the work in text (TXT) with no formatting, since this can be read by all modern word processing software, as well as DOS.

Providing your copy on disk cuts down on the editor's work—since there is no retyping required. Offering dual formats ensures that your text will be easy to read and manipulate. If you are sending articles by e-mail, there are also special requirements. For instance, should your work be sent as an attachment or as text in the body of the message? Again, it is always best to ask the editor if she does not specify.

More complex is the question of digital images and graphics. Most, but not all, printing operations today have gone digital, meaning they can read common picture files (JPG, GIF, TIF, etc.) from a computer disk. Not all editors and art directors, however, have the capability to view such images. As a result, they require that pictures be submitted in traditional formats (color slides and/or prints). Slowly, though, the editorial world is coming around.

"I really like your 'Philippine Jungle Adventure' article," Cindy Alpers, editor of the Internet magazine *Tropi-Ties,* wrote recently, "but I cannot use it unless you can provide digital images."

The same week, James Randall, editor of Mobil Oil's *Compass,* faxed to tell me that "Unfortunately, we cannot use images from a disk. We need slides or prints."

These two extremes illustrate the state of contemporary publishing. There are still mom-and-pop operations out there that work on a shoestring. At the same time, there are ultramodern publications that require all material in digital format, transmitted by Internet, and ready to print. The future of the publishing industry lies with the latter. For now, though, play it safe with your packaging and *always* ask the editor if electronic submissions and the inclusion of computer disk with text and images would be helpful. If the answer is yes, then by all means take the additional time and effort required to provide them. If, on the other hand, you are told no, you will have increased the editor's respect for your professionalism by offering such a service.

Courier Delivery

Whenever possible, I send editorial material electronically. Such delivery saves time and dramatically reduces the overhead of shipping. When a package must go by "snail mail," however, I set that little creature on a rocket by using courier services exclusively.

There are several reasons why you should always use courier service or express mail to deliver your work. First and foremost is the speed in which packages arrive. Much of the editorial work you do will be timely. This means that it should reach the editor's hands as soon as possible. Even when deadlines are not a factor, getting the completed product to the editor quickly will make a good impression as well as get you paid that much faster.

Utilizing courier service also maintains your "big business" image. I know of no company that sends important documents via traditional postal methods. And, in my view, there is nothing more important than the work that generates the money on which I live. For this reason, I opened an account with UPS seven years ago. By having an account, I receive lower rates than I would normally have to pay at UPS pickup points. Additionally, the contract guarantees that the courier will retrieve packages from my home or office, saving me time. All I do is call the toll-free number for next day pickup. As a business, you also have the advantage of paying on receipt of an invoice.

The final reason I suggest using courier service or express mail is the Internet tracking systems provided by these companies. I did some work recently for *Pacific Stars and Stripes* in Japan, and sent it by UPS. A month later, I received a message asking when I would have the material completed. Going to the UPS Tracking Internet page *(www.ups.com/tracking/tracking.html)* was able to view every movement of this shipment from the time it left my office until it was signed for at the receiving end, simply by inserting the Way Bill number. I then sent an e-mail to the editor saying, "On November 17, Becky Johnson signed for the material." Within an hour the editor had the package, and I had an apology.

UPS is not the only company offering online tracking. Here are others for your reference:

Airborne Express—
www.airborne-express.com/trace/trace.htm

DHL—*www.dhl.com/track/track.html*

Emery Worldwide—
www.emeryworld.com/track/eww_trac.html

Federal Express—*www.fedex.com/us/tracking*

U.S. Postal Service—(for Express Mail only)—
www.usps.gov/cttgate

Customer Service/ Satisfaction

Many business empires have been built on superb customer service and satisfaction. And yet, these two words—*customer service*—are rarely, if ever, part of a writer's business vocabulary. The true guerrilla marketer takes advantage of customer service, turning it into multiple sales and an expanded clientele. But satisfying customers is more than a post-assignment task. It should begin with your initial approach, or query, and span the entire length of your business relationship.

I began thinking customer service many years ago when I received a message from the founding editor of *Robb Report*. It read: "We never give assignments to writers with whom we have not worked previously." Taking him at his word, I wrote my first story for this slick, monthly magazine on spec. I was confident that I could produce a feature he would love. I was wrong. Fortunately, he was one of those rare breeds of editors willing to nurture talented writers and gave me a second shot. Detailing the specific problems he had with the original piece, he asked for a rewrite. The result was "Tuscany Trails," a four-page spread that netted me $800.

Though the editor has since retired, I have gone on to write other stories for *Robb Report*. The lesson learned from that first sale, however, forever influenced the way I do business. Whenever I pitch an idea to a newspaper or magazine for which I have never worked, I always offer to do the article on speculation. The reason? In most cases, the editor has no idea with whom he is corresponding or whether I am capable of producing a feature that matches his readership. Offering to write the story with no obligation gives the editor a guarantee. I am basically saying that "I will ensure your satisfaction, or you pay nothing."

Many professional writers' organizations—including the American Society of Journalists and Authors, of which I am currently a member of the Board of Directors—disagree with writers doing work on a noncontract basis. Yet I believe that perhaps 75 percent or more of these organizations' members operate this way. The rigid competition for freelance writing assignments today requires us to accept on-spec work if we are to make a living. Writers who insist on contract work and consider on-spec writing a sign of lowering their professional standards are often staff writers. I prefer to look at it from a marketing standpoint. Doing a story at no obligation is merely offering a guarantee. It is customer service at its best. More than this, it is opening new roads to future business. It is a marketing tactic—step one so to speak—on the way to reaching those coveted contracted assignments.

The Italians have a saying that fits this situation perfectly: *"Chi non risica, non rosica."* While this translates to "Who doesn't risk, doesn't eat," the concept is that if you never try, you are never going to achieve anything. (Our more pedestrian expression for the same idea is "Nothing ventured, nothing gained.") That is why I write on spec—because it has allowed me, and can allow you, to make some great achievements. This technique has given me the opportunity to break into several national publications that, otherwise, might have rejected my queries. It enhances my chances of getting a green light from editors with whom I have never worked. Two months ago, for instance, I sent an e-mail query to Mark Walter, editor of *The Seybold Report on Internet Publishing*, a monthly trade publication. My interest in the magazine was twofold: (1) I had recently done a short feature on the Web site of Italian fashion house Diesel, which I felt could be expanded to fit Seybold's needs and (2) they paid $1,000 to $3,000.

Walter thought that the idea sounded interesting, but replied: "I can't commission you to do it (because we have never worked with you), but I will pay for any story you submit that we publish. Once we get beyond the first story, we could work on a longer-term and more regular relationship."

The completed article appeared in the February 1999 issue of *The Seybold Report on Internet Publishing* and brought me $1,500. Mark and I are now discussing a long-term, regular contributor relationship.

"There is no need to work on spec for future work," explained Walter, "We'll provide guaranteed assignments."

When writing on spec, my thinking is that should the editor ultimately *not* buy the story, I can always sell it elsewhere. At the same time, though, I make one stipulation in my "no obligation" approach. That is, I insist that if the editor is not pleased with the completed article, I will be given the opportunity to do one rewrite. In the past fifteen years I have had to use this option only three times—and in only one case did the editor ultimately not buy the revised version.

Accepting All Jobs

Another aspect of editorial customer service is accepting jobs that you are not always enthusiastic about. Currently, I am writing a feature on European motorcycle riding for *R&R Magazine*, published in Germany. It seems the advertising department was given a truckload of money from Harley-Davidson. As a result, the motorcycle-theme article was scheduled for the July issue. There was only one problem: The editor had no one to write the story.

When I was thirteen, I was in a motorcycle accident. That ended my interest in two-wheel vehicles. Because I have been selling articles to *R&R Magazine* for twenty years, however, I was more than willing to help the editor when her plea came in. Why? Not because I needed the stress of the tight deadline, nor the mediocre fee that the magazine pays, but because it was my "duty" as a professional to assist the editor when she needed it most. That is a true commitment to customer satisfaction.

All marketers realize that you cannot satisfy everyone. Customers who are pleased with your work, however, should be nurtured—cultivated like a rare plant. These individuals will be the mainstays of your future income. In fact, recent studies indicate that 80 percent of a business' income normally comes from 20 percent of its clients. It is only natural, therefore, that you would want to focus most of your efforts and customer service on this 20 percent, while opening new avenues of income by continuously adding new clients.

When you take your car to a mechanic and receive poor service, undoubtedly, you will never return. If you receive fast, reliable service, on the other hand, chances are excellent that you'll be back. Fortunately, you do not have to wait for a client's next oil change to gain additional work. In fact, you need to strike while the iron is still hot.

Upon completion of an article, a speech, a corporate brochure, a newsletter, a book, a seminar, or any other type of work, you should immediately be thinking of new ideas for this client. The book you are reading is an excellent example. Following the publication of *The Writer's and Photographer's Guide to Global Markets* (Allworth Press), I immediately queried publisher Tad Crawford for a book on aggressive sales tactics for writers. Based on the writing and the professional way in which the first book was presented—including beating the deadline by forty days—we were able to come to an agreement for the second title within two weeks.

> "Accompany each article that you submit with a list of new story ideas. You might as well land your next assignment while you're on a roll. Use each accomplishment as a stepping-stone to the next. The moment I wrote my first piece for a national magazine, I could add 'published in national magazines' to my bio. The moment my first book hit the bookstore shelves, I could trumpet the fact that I was a 'published author.' These days, I'm announcing the fact that I've written six books in a little over a year—one of which has been chosen as a Book of the Month Club selection. Bottom line? Use each achievement to leverage the next."
> —*Ann Douglas, author of* The Unofficial Guide to Childcare

Ask for More

If you have written and sold an article to a publication, this is the time to propose a continuous relationship. In most cases, contributing editors, correspondents, and even some associate editors are nothing more than freelance writers who have successfully become part of the magazine's stable of writers. They are also the ones producing most of the features—and receiving the largest percentage of the company's editorial budget. Getting yourself on the masthead and among the ranks of regular contributors should be your ultimate goal if you write articles.

During the past two decades, I have proposed myself as a contributing editor to over 120 newspapers and magazines. I've been successful about 10 percent of the time. My name has appeared on the masthead of *Armed Forces Journal International, Cardiology World News, Diplomat, Family, International Daily News, International Living, Internet.com, Off Duty, Scientific American Archaeology,* and *Writer On Line,* just to mention a few. I have been a travel editor, a technology editor, a foreign correspondent, and a bureau chief. Titles aside, I was basically a freelance writer assigned a weekly or monthly feature or column. In one case, I eventually wrote three columns—one on photography, one on cooking, a third on travel—under different names.

The main point here is that you should take the initiative to propose yourself as a regular contributor as soon as you've successfully sold an article and ensured that the client is pleased with your work. Oftentimes, this means coming up with a niche that is not already filled by another writer. Having just written and sold my first story to Mark Walter at *The Seybold Report on Internet Publishing,* for instance, I am now putting together a proposal for a long-term, continuing relationship under which I will cover European Web sites. Because the magazine is published and distributed in the United States, I assumed that most of its writers are also located in America. This gives me an advantage. After reviewing several copies of the publication, my thoughts were confirmed—nearly every article focused on domestic Web publishing.

In my proposal, I will offer my services on a monthly basis and provide a list of the first four features I intend to write. Each idea will consist of a one-paragraph "pitch," giving the editor sufficient information to understand the theme of each story. At worst, the editor will turn down the proposal. At best, it will bring me steady, monthly work and increase my annual income by $18,000 to $36,000.

When putting together your own "contributor" proposals, always keep marketing in mind: What does the editor need? How can I help the publication generate revenue through my features? What niche market is the publication missing? A good way to do this is to pretend that you are the publisher. As such, your job is to generate money by increasing your advertising. Review a few recent issues of the magazine. Ask yourself, what niches are being overlooked? Where can we expand our readership? Or advertising? Or editorial? In the case of *The Seybold Report on Internet Publishing*, my answer was simple: The publication would grow by reaching European readers and markets. Thus, I proposed my services in that area—pointing out the potential for increased advertising sales and readership.

Even when writing under assignment, or contract, you should offer the client a guarantee. This is particularly important for corporate work. The kill fee option—when clients offer to pay a percentage (normally 20–25 percent) of the agreed price if they are not satisfied with your work—is the best way to handle this. It gives the client an option to pull out of the deal, but ensures that you will receive some compensation for your time and effort.

If you are like most writers, you approach an editor whenever you've come up with an idea that seems right for her. Guerrilla marketers, including myself, will tell you that that is not the way to operate a successful business. Working this way, you are in the editor's mind, in most cases, only when you send her something. What you want to do is be in her mind constantly—and you want those thoughts to always be positive. The reason for this is very simple—continued work. Over the past three months, four editors have called me with assignments. Why? Because I was the first person they thought of when they needed a writer.

Gifts and Goodies

To achieve this "ever-present" status, I take a series of actions to stimulate repeat business as well as enhance my company's visibility. As I've mentioned, in many completed article packages, I include discount coupons. While the returns are not overwhelming, I have achieved fair success with specially focused offers such as these, particularly toward the end of the year when editors are normally strapped for funds. I maintain a list of customers and periodically send them small gifts (which highlight the Strawberry Media name and address) or promotional mailings (more about these in chapter 7).

One of the most productive freebee marketing products I've developed has been a customized disk of computer screen-saver backgrounds. Because I work with some excellent photographers, I asked each of them to contribute one of their most dramatic images for promotional use. It was then a simple task to merge a promotional text message over the image with Corel Draw—there are several other programs that work, too. As part of the message, I included both the company and my name and contact information. Next, I saved five of these "Computer Billboards" onto a floppy disk and sent them, along with instructions on how to apply them as monitor backgrounds, to my client list.

It took only two weeks before the thank-you letters began to arrive. One client—a university administrator—

said, "Great screen backgrounds! Thanks! I've gotten a lot of comments on the volcano image since I configured it into my computer. The best thing, though, is that I won't have to go digging any more when I need to contact you."

Everyone likes to get freebees and, if they increase your business, you should dedicate time and resources to such items. It is important, however, that you always focus on items that will keep you and your company consistently in the minds of your clients.

THE BATTLE PLAN

*L*ike anything done well, marketing requires planning. Setting out on a marketing venture without a precise plan is like taking a trip without a map; you can make right turns and left turns but never seem to reach your final destination. Therefore, the more precise you are in your planning, the easier it will be to reach your goals.

The first factor in any marketing plan is a budget. Without knowing how much you have, or are willing to spend, it is impossible to prepare a working strategy. Without allocating a specific sum of money to your plan, what you are doing, in effect, is dreaming of what you would "like" to do, rather than focusing on what is realistically possible. Strange as it may seem, I have worked with many of today's Fortune 500 companies and had the marketing directors say:

"Prepare a marketing plan for us, then we'll see if we have the funds to cover it."

Why is money so important? Just as a battle commander with a limited number of soldiers can protect only a certain amount of territory, a marketing director with a restricted budget can only spread the word so far. Let's say, for example, that you plan to do a mailing to editors of fifty travel magazines. If your package is professionally done, the postage alone might cost over $200. After you have purchased stationery, presentation folders, and copied clips of published works to include in the package, if you don't have the $200 for postage, what you are doing is simply spinning your wheels, dreaming. So be realistic about your goals and your expectations based on your budget.

There are ways to cut costs and still carry out a highly professional marketing operation. Using the Internet is an excellent way to dramatically decrease overhead. Samples of your work can be scanned and transmitted as e-mail attachments, or you can direct potential clients to your Web page. Another method of lowering marketing costs is to create an introductory brochure for your services and products. These can be generated at local print shops for very low cost and, if designed correctly, will fit perfectly into a standard envelope. Be sure, however, that the paper stock you use does not exceed the 1-ounce, first class mail weight limit.

While you do not want to waste money, you also do not want to be so tight with your cash that it hinders quality. Keep in mind that after you have made the decision to treat your writing as a business, you must then set aside a fixed amount of funds for marketing purposes. This budget, or lack thereof, will determine how your plan is laid out and executed.

For the most part, writers should operate two parallel marketing plans: the first to sell their work, the second to sell themselves. While each area has its own specific focus and scope, they will generally overlap. Each time you publish an article or book, you are, in a sense, marketing yourself. Too few writers understand and take advantage of this fact—missing out on the promotional benefits of having their name in print. Those who do profit from this area are often the writers you see on such programs as *Good Morning America* discussing topics that range from child care and home financing to world affairs and the president's legal woes.

A recent episode of the *Today* show perfectly illustrated this point. A writer who had recently produced a feature on stock market trends for *Money Magazine* was advising viewers to ride out Wall Street's current downswing caused by global economic events. Given the number of people who watch *Today*, more than one book editor or publisher was likely listening to this individual. One, or more, in fact, may very well have been thinking: Trends on Wall Street—that would make a good book. He then may have made a mental note to call the magazine for the writer's telephone number. Such things happen more frequently than you might expect.

"Don't go overboard and dilute your efforts by trying to do everything at once."
—*John Kremer,* 1001 Ways to Market Your Books

While laying out and executing a dual-marketing plan, the basic logistics may be much the same. Stationery, business cards, and samples of published works will be required in both cases. If you have followed the advice given in previous chapters, you're prepared in this area and have a media kit ready.

Keep It Simple

There is nothing difficult about a marketing plan, though I've known many corporate marketing directors who like to make it seem so to justify their well-paying positions. For me it is a matter of Q+C=S. That is, Query plus Consistency equals Success. I begin by focusing on a target market. Say your goal is to sell two travel articles each month. To achieve this, do your market research using as many methods outlined in previous chapters as possible, then send out one query a week—always on a different subject, but within the travel theme. At the end of one month, you will have four queries out. At the same time, maintain a list of publications where you can send ideas should they come back rejected. To expand your efforts—and use the shotgun submission method—try sending each query out to five markets around the world (each one targeting a different country).

Eventually, assignments will come in. Don't stop your marketing efforts, though. This is where the "C" or consistency comes into play. Keep sending out a new query each week. Utilizing this method, I found myself, after three years, with over 250 queries out and more than twenty assignments at any given time. I ultimately stopped using the Q+C=S method because I could not keep up with the work flow—a position I hope you will soon find yourself in.

This same strategy can be applied to book sales as well. In this case, however, you will be sending out one book query a week, followed by a complete proposal. Because I have tried to focus more energy on book writing over the past year, I began this systematic method several months ago. Today I have more than sixty queries and twenty-three book proposals out.

The Q+C=S plan can also be applied to self-promotion. It should, in fact, be incorporated into your marketing of articles, books, and services. If you find it too difficult to maintain the pace—and eventually you should—then divide your efforts between marketing of products and marketing of yourself. For instance, week one send out queries for articles, week two send out self-promotional media kits. Alternating weeks will keep you stimulated and also allow time for your mind to think of new ideas and markets.

You may be asking why you can't simply do a mass mailing of your media kit. You could. There are several problems with this method, however. First, marketing costs would be high at the beginning of your campaign, rather than spread out over a period of time. Second, you might experience a rush of interest, then, six months later, find yourself sitting alone with no work and no media interest in you or what you have to say. For these reasons, your efforts should be precisely targeted and consistent. Don't let a week go by without doing something to sell your work and market yourself.

Though I am always looking for opportunities, I maintain a monthly and annual list to ensure that nothing is forgotten. It is now, for instance, February. My list says: (1) week one—query ten newspapers around the world (same query to each) on Summer Cruises in the Mediterranean; (2) week two—send media kit to ten TV producers, offer to speak on Archaeological Travel; (3) week three—send book query to ten publishers in New York, topic: Archaeological Travel Guide Series; (4) week four—September is back to school month, send media kit to ten universities and offer my services as a seminar instructor. Query women's magazines on Living through the Back-to-School Crisis.

This very simple, one-line plan keeps me on track. As ideas and projects come to mind, I add them to the list. The result is a constantly growing, developing marketing plan that is easy to follow and can be altered, if necessary, based on daily developments.

The key is to have a written "map" to follow on weekly and monthly bases. Make sure that all your efforts fit the budget you've set aside. And, most important, maintain a consistent plan to sell your work and yourself.

5 x 5 Matrix Marketing Plan

When asked what a marketing plan should be like, author and publisher John Kremer pointed out that it should take into consideration the potential audiences, how you plan to reach these target markets, the price of your product and/or services, and what you expect to gain from sales—that is, your financial benefit.

"When I generate a plan," says Kremer, "I use a 5 × 5 matrix marketing plan. I list five major audiences for my book (or service), prioritized 1 to 5. Then under each of these five audiences, I list the five major ways I plan to reach each of them. I start by brainstorming lots of ways. Then I select the five best ways—as determined by what I think I can actually achieve—due to restrictions in my time, money, and other resources."

Here, in these few words, lies the concept behind all marketing plans. Kremer goes one step further, however, to point out that, from this matrix, a time line must be projected, taking into account lead times. For example, if you were trying to sell articles on winter sports, you would not want to market them in October or November, due to the required lead time. Similarly, trying to sell a seminar is best done several months before you would like to begin. This will give the organizer sufficient time to prepare his own promotional campaign for your class.

In general, you should allow at least six months' lead time for magazines, whereas newspapers can often work within a one-week window.

"Radio shows," says Kremer, "vary from about a week to one month . . . Within this time line, I prioritize the activities that I believe will provide me with the best return on my company's investment of time and resources."

ODDS 'N' ENDS

Many aspects of good marketing do not fall into specific categories or under hard, fast headings. Some things can be applied to a single, target market, while others overlap and can be applied to all your efforts. One thing that does remain constant, however, is the necessity to make every idea and every tactic your own. Don't simply copy the methods in this book. Personalize them. Allow them to fit your specific needs. Whether you are trying to sell an article, a book, a speech, a service, or yourself, marketing is your responsibility and no one else's. It is also up to you to develop your own style and approach.

"Success breeds new opportunity for success."
—*Rush Limbaugh, author of* The Way Things Ought To Be

Once you get into the swing of guerrilla marketing, you'll find that the river of opportunity flows endlessly. Today's efforts will grow like wildflowers, creating the opportunities of tomorrow. To ensure that you take full advantage of this cycle of promotion, I'd like to share some tips from Joan Stewart, a media relations speaker, trainer, and consultant, who also publishes *The Publicity Hound,* a bimonthly newsletter featuring tips, tricks, and tools for free—or really cheap—publicity (see the appendix).

Fourteen Ways to Recycle Publicity
—by Joan Stewart ©

Feeling proud for persuading a local radio station to air a half-hour interview with you? Or for getting a two-page spread about your new book (or yourself) in a national magazine?

If you're an amateur publicity hound, you're content with whatever you can get. If you're a pro, however, you know the fun is just beginning, because the challenge is to turn one media "hit" into multiple hits. Here are fourteen ways independent publishers (and writers) can recycle publicity:

1. Several days before you appear on a radio show, send a postcard to bookstores, newspapers, or magazine reporters—or anyone else who should listen to the show. Tell them the time, date, and where to find the show on the dial.

2. When you do a radio interview about a book (an article, a service, or yourself), ask the host off the air, "Who else do you know who might be interested in having me as a guest?" Talk show hosts often have valuable contacts in other markets.

3. Tape the talk show. Give copies of the tape to print reporters who you want to write about you, and slip a copy of the cassette inside your media kit.

4. Reprint newspaper and magazine stories about you, with permission. Add them to existing marketing materials, use them as leave-behinds if you do bookstore appearances, and distribute them at speaking engagements. Larger newspapers and magazines have their own reprint services.

5. Recycle stories from the print media by including them on your Web site, with permission. If it's a snazzy, helpful site, send an e-mail to publications like *USA Today* that "review" Web sites and ask them to take a look.

6. If a national publication prints a story by or about you or your book (or service), write a short news release about it for your daily and weekly newspapers, trade publications, chamber of commerce newsletter, and alumni magazine. That's what I did when *PR Tactics,* a national newspaper for the public relations industry, printed an article I wrote last fall. A reporter at a local weekly saw my news release, called me for an interview, wrote a half-page story about my business, and included a photo.

7. Write a letter to the editor of the publication that just printed a story about you. Discuss one or two points the reporter didn't include, or elaborate on a specific issue. Use this same technique when your competitor gets ink and you don't. Write a letter to the editor or a longer opinion piece on whatever the topic is about. Include a photo.

8. Invite reporters to workshops you are presenting. A local reporter attended a half-day workshop I presented through the local chamber of commerce on how to get free publicity. She wrote a front-page story about it. I made reprints of the story for my own media kit.

9. Don't forget newspaper and magazine columnists, who always need fresh ideas. Rather than asking them to write about you, invite them to one of your presentations. Or ask them to lunch.

10. If you do public speaking, offer to write a short article summarizing your speech for the group's newsletter. Don't forget to offer your photo.

11. Use radio talk shows to promote upcoming book signings, workshops, classes you are teaching, or other appearances in the community.

12. Send reprints of weekly newspaper stories by and about you to editors at dailies. Send reprints from dailies to national publications. Send articles in trade publications to editors anywhere.

13. If you are a guest on an out-of-town radio or TV show, call the newspaper in the city where the show is airing and ask if they would like an interview too.

14. Include a page in your media kit or on your Web site listing all media appearances by category (radio, TV, newspaper, magazines) and update it regularly. Send the list, along with your "pitch" letter, to editors, reporters, and news directors, to let them know you aren't a media novice.

(reprinted from SPAN Connection,
with permission of the author)

Spoofs

Getting media coverage can sometimes be difficult unless you come up with a unique story angle. Writer Alan Caruba discovered this in the early 1980s. After a while, in fact, he became bored with the entire process. Little did he realize that his emotional state would be the key to his future success.

"The Boring Institute *(www.boringinstitute.com)* began as a spoof of media hype," he recalls, "and continues with that purpose today. In 1984, I put out a news release, inventing the institute, saying that it had concluded that the Macy's Thanksgiving Day Parade was, in fact, a ten-year-old videotape. It received an immediate response and, the next month, I initiated the first list of 'The Most Boring Celebrities of the Year' as a spoof of all the end of the year lists of who's hot and who's not. It was an instant hit."

As a result of his "boring" spoof, Caruba made news across America, appearing on many of television's most popular talk shows, doing radio spots, and gaining coverage in *Newsweek, Time, People,* and *USA Today.* Today his "Most Boring . . ." lists continue to come out annually and he has become an international personality. To ensure year-round visibility in the news, he releases a spoof of the Academy Awards in the spring, a midyear serious look at boredom's impact on people's lives, and, in the fall, a commentary on the hideous new television shows.

"The institute gives me name recognition and opens the door to many people in the media who, in fact, seek me out," Caruba says.

Alan's is a story of how a single writer, with intelligence and a bit of marketing know-how, can gain recognition without writing a best-selling book. By breaking away from traditional molds—even using spoofs—you can always stay one step ahead of the crowd. And the more name recognition you generate, the more popular you become, and the more publishers will want you. So be creative.

"I do think that writers need to promote themselves every time anything they do gets in print," suggests Caruba. "Send out a release about the article, send copies of it to other media. Develop a reputation for speaking about your area of expertise on radio and TV. That sort of thing. The more famous you become, the more leverage you may have with editors."

Answering Machine Marketing

There is a thing in the movie business called a "log-line." If you ever get an opportunity to pitch a story to a producer the first thing she will probably ask is, "What's the log-line?" That is, what's your story in a condensed version of, say, two or three sentences.

Prior to calling a potential market to pitch a book, an article, a corporate contract, a seminar, a lecture, or any other service or product, always prepare a log-line. Phrase your idea in a clear but concise way. By doing this, you will have a script to guide you through your spiel once the prospective client has answered your call.

In the event that you reach an answering machine, record the pitch for the client to hear upon his return. If he likes it, you'll get a return call. On the other hand, if you simply ask for a return call, you'll probably never hear from him.

More Free Tips

I like to periodically explore what others are suggesting when it comes to marketing. After all, no one has ever had all the answers. An Internet site I check from time to time— Herman Holtz's *Tips for Marketing*—offers great insights that can be incorporated into my own methods of business. Most ideas from this source revolve around the theme of how to make more money writing and becoming a consultant— which is a natural extension for many niche writers. Check it out at *www.bellicose.com/freelance.*

A popular, free, e-mail newsletter that focuses on marketing and the Internet is *Image World,* edited by Robert Zee. The people behind this publication believe that small and large businesses can all thrive via new digital technologies, and I cannot argue that point. To subscribe, send an e-mail to: *subscribe@imageworld.net.* The Web site *(http://imageworld.net)* includes the one hundred–plus best places to promote your Web site for free.

Editor Night

New York writer Leil Lowndes says that "There are more good writers than editors can use. The ones who market are the ones who get contracts."

To ensure that he is one of the elite scribes who are consistently employed, Leil has initiated a unique technique, which you might want to duplicate. He holds "Evenings with Editors" at his loft in SoHo that, in turn, enhances his personal relationship with editors of top publications.

Lowndes makes contact with assignment editors at some well-paying magazines based in New York City and invites them to attend an evening session to talk with writers about their needs and guidelines. Once he has confirmed an editor and a date, he then invites twenty-five to thirty writers.

"This gives me direct contact with editors," he says.

Collecting What's Due

Most writers of articles, sooner or later, come across a client that either delays payment or, in some cases, never pays. While many professional organizations advise their members to take such clients to court, the cost involved in this process often does not justify the effort. For example, let's say a magazine owes you $250. Even in small claims court, it may cost you this much or more in time, paperwork, and communications to pursue legal action.

There is, however, a trick you can try for clients that fall into this nonpaying category if they have e-mail. You simply create an e-mail letter to a fictitious collection agency, copying the editor and anyone else at the publication who has influence on getting you paid. Here is my message:

> To: jcook@usacollection.com
> From: msedge@aol.com
> Cc: dedwards@nopaymag.com
>   Jsimon@nopaymag.com

> Dear Mr. Cook,
> In reference to our telephone conversation of today, I am sending, by Federal Express, the documentation related to the nonpayment of $250.00 by *No Pay Magazine* for editorial services provided by myself for the January issue of this publication. The terms discussed for USA Collection Agency to handle the recovery of this payment are acceptable. I look forward to hearing from you on this matter and thank you for your assistance.

> Sincerely,

> Michael Sedge
> Strawberry Media

When you send the message it will be returned to you with an error message because the credit agency does not exist. The publication, however, does not know this. The editors and others there have received their copy of the message and, at this point, should be sweating and/or cutting you a check.

I have used this technique successfully in two cases. Unless a publication is going bankrupt, it should draw an immediate response. Why? Because one of the first actions a collection agency takes is to place the person or company owing money on a "bad credit" list, which is circulated nationally. Therefore, should the publication apply for credit of any type—from a bank loan to a calling card—it raises a red flag, which often results in rejection. Eventually, if not paid, a bad debt could affect the publication's permanent credit record.

When I introduced this technique recently to a newsgroup of the American Society of Journalist and Authors, I was slammed by some members who called it "terrible advice" while others praised me and asked if they could pass it on to other writers' organizations. Whether you use it or not is up to you. My feeling on this is that any method that will allow me to recover money, no matter how small the amount, is worth a try.

> "Marketing is everything. I've often wished I could sit at my computer all day and do nothing but write, but then I am reminded of an old saying, 'Writing without selling is like acting without applause.'"
> —*Lynn Grisard Fullman, professional writer*

Corporate Cooperation

I have worked for MCI Communications, Holiday Inn, H&R Block, and Rapid Link Telecommunications. While the pay for corporate work is often better than average—when compared to articles and nonfiction books—there is also reluctance on the part of many companies to offer work to outsiders. I've been able to overcome this hurdle, however, by offering to work under a "fee plus percentage" payment arrangement.

For example, Holiday Inn paid me a fixed fee to write marketing material, then, for a one-year period, a commission (10 percent) on all the business resulting from the press kits, releases, and brochures I created. We assigned a booking code to all materials, which allowed me—and them—to constantly know the results of my work (a standard marketing technique).

At the end of the year, 271 rooms had been booked in connection with the promotional material. At $120 a night, that was $32,520. I took home $3,252, plus the initial $700.

In the case of MCI, I produced press materials—and as well distributed them—and received a monthly commission on new customer telephone usage. Let's say, for example, the marketing director and I decided to promote the MCI WorldPhone calling card to U.S. military members in Japan. I would create press releases and other marketing tools. MCI would foot the bill for expenses and pay me $500. When customers applied for the service, a tracking code would be assigned that linked the customer back to my efforts. As the client began calling, I would get a monthly commission—between 5 and 7 percent—based on the billed amount. Did it work? Let's just say that I am currently getting monthly checks that exceed $1,000.

Moral of the story? Be creative when approaching corporations. You may find that you can land more work and more money if you ask yourself, "How can I help this company get more clients?"

Don't Overlook the Obvious

Sometimes the obvious is easy to overlook when you are focusing on tricks and techniques to market yourself, your products, and your services. This morning, as I was putting the finishing touches on the first draft of this book, my phone rang.

"Mr. Sedge?"

"Yes."

"This is Marco Guerra, from *La Republica* in Rome. During a recent trip to the United States, I read the interview you did with Tom Clancy. We're interested in using the article in Italian, if reprint rights are available."

"Excellent," I say. "But, I am curious. How did you find me?"

"At the end of the article, it said you live in Naples. I simply looked you up in the Yellow Pages."

Yes. I have a tiny, box ad in the Yellow Pages under Journalist . . . and so should every professional writer.

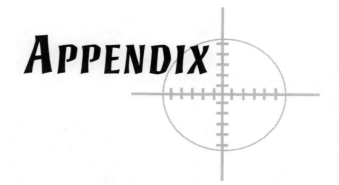

APPENDIX

RESOURCES FOR THE WARRIOR WRITER

Associations and Organizations

ASJA (American Society of Journalists and Authors, Inc.)
1501 Broadway, Suite 302, New York, NY 10036
Tel: (212) 997-0947
Fax: (212) 768-7414
E-mail: *asja@compuserve.com*
Web: *www.asja.org*

ASJA is an organization of professional nonfiction writers. The association has a network of regional chapters and sponsors monthly as well as annual events. Annual membership includes a monthly newsletter, listing in the ASJA Membership Directory, and numerous services of value to the working writer.

SPAN (Small Publishers Association of North America)
P.O. Box 1306, 425 Cedar Street, Buena Vista, CO 81211-1306
Tel: (719) 395-4790
Fax: (719) 395-8374

E-mail: *SPAN@SPANnet.org.*
Web: *www.SPANnet.org.*

SPAN is a group of America's finest small publishers. Members receive the monthly *SPAN Connection* newsletter, an annual directory of small publishers, discounts on book marketing opportunities, and a vast array of other information and services for selling books and other products.

Publications

Big Ideas for Small Service Businesses
Authored by veteran marketers Marilyn and Tom Ross, this title provides a wealth of marketing strategies for any business. $15.95. Communications Creativity, P.O. Box 909, Buena Vista, CO 81211-0909. Tel: (800) 331-8355.

Book Marketing Update
A twice-a-month, eight-page newsletter with marketing tips for authors and publishers, including print and broadcast media, as well as an array of other promotional tips. $247.00 a year. Bradley Communications Corp., 135 East Plumstead Avenue, P.O. Box 1206, Lansdowne, PA 19050-8206. Tel: (800) 989-1400.

Bradley's Guide to the Top National TV Talk Shows
Find out who picks guests for Larry King. Learn how to get on *Good Morning America, Oprah, Montel,* and much, much more. $75.00. Bradley Communications Corp., 135 East Plumstead Avenue, P.O. Box 1206, Lansdowne, PA 19050-8206. Tel: (800) 989-1400.

The Complete Guide to Book Marketing
All aspects of book marketing are covered in this comprehensive resource by David Cole. Learn how to build a publishing identity, target an audience and cultivate feedback from it, establish distributor partnerships, and develop publicity and public relations strategies. $19.95. Allworth Press, 10 E. 23rd Street, Suite 210, New York, NY 10010. Tel: (212) 777-8395.

Empire Building
This is a how-to guide by Gordon Burgett for entrepreneurs looking to build or enhance their business through writing and speaking. $12.95. Communications Unlimited, P.O. Box 6405, Santa Maria, CA 93456. Tel: (800) 563-1454.

Essential Business Tactics for the Net
If you are new to Internet business and marketing, check out this title by Larry Chase. $29.99. John Wiley & Sons, 605 Third Avenue, New York, NY 10158-0012. Tel: (800) ALL-BOOK.

Getting Business to Come to You
The perfect resource for small businesses, by Paul and Sarah Edwards and Laura Clampitt Douglas. Second edition, $18.95. Putnam Publishing Group, 200 Madison Avenue, New York, NY 10016. Tel: (212) 951-8400.

How to Sell Products via the Internet
An excellent, twenty-page report. $5.00. Open Horizons, P.O. Box 205, Fairfield, IA 52556-0205. Tel: (800) 796-6130.

How to Set Up and Market Your Own Seminars
Gordon Burgett does a great, step-by-step job of telling you how to jump into the lucrative seminar business. Audiotape set, 180 minutes, and a twenty-six–page workbook. $44.95. Communications Unlimited, P.O. Box 6405, Santa Maria, CA 93456. Tel: (800) 563-1454.

Jump-Start Your Book Sales
While focusing on book sales, the advice given by authors Marilyn and Tom Ross can be applied to all forms of marketing. $23.95. Communication Creativity, P.O. Box 909, Buena Vista, CO 81211-0909. Tel: (800) 331-8355.

Niche Marketing
If you want to make yourself indispensable as a writer and speaker, this title will help you achieve this goal. $14.95. Authored by Gordon Burgett. Communications Unlimited, P.O. Box 6405, Santa Maria, CA 93456. Tel: (800) 563-1454.

The Publicity Hound

This bimonthly newsletter features tips, tricks, and tools to obtain free (or really cheap) publicity. Written by Joan Stewart. $49.95 for U.S. subscription, $59.95 outside the United States Sample copy $3. Send check to The Publicity Hound, 3920 Highway O, Saukville, WI 53080. Tel: (414) 284-7451. E-mail: *jstewart@execpc.com.*

Publisher's Weekly

Keep up with people in the publishing industry with this weekly trade magazine. Fifty-one issues a year, $169.00. Publisher's Weekly, P.O. Box 6457, Torrance, CA 90504-0457. Tel: (800) 278-2991.

1001 Ways to Market Your Books

This has been called the bible of book marketing. Tips can be applied to all forms of sales, however. Authored by publishing veteran John Kremer, $27.95. Open Horizons, P.O. Box 205, Fairfield, IA 52556-0205. Tel: (800) 796-6130.

Web Marketing Cookbook

This is a book/CD combination providing over twenty ready-to-use templates for site design, searching, viewing, and the like. It is subtitled "All the Ingredients You Need to Implement a Five Star Electronic Marketing Strategy" and delivers on this claim. $39.99. John Wiley & Sons, 605 Third Avenue, New York, NY 10158-0012.

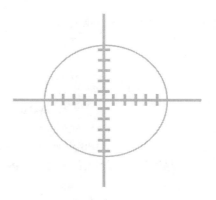

ABOUT THE AUTHOR

In the 1980s, Michael Sedge learned that he could sell more and gain more respect in the publishing industry by working under an agency heading. Thus began the Strawberry Media Agency. Most of his many publishing credits—more than 2,600 articles and several books—have been sold through this one-man marketing/editorial operation.

A long-time self-syndication wizard, Sedge's clients span a wide geographic range, from Cape Town to Chicago, Houston to Heidelberg, Manila to Manchester, and Sydney to Singapore. His success in article placement led to his self-published book, *Double Your Income through Foreign and Reprint Sales* and the recently released *The Writer's and Photographer's Guide to Global Markets* (Allworth Press).

Recognizing his talent for marketing books, Para Publishing commissioned Sedge to produce *Selling Books to the Military Market*.

Because of his vast knowledge of the publishing industry, Michael Sedge has written extensively on selling articles, books, and scripts to such publications as *Authorlink, Authorship, Byline, Income Opportunities, Inkling, Markets Abroad, NovelAdvice, Photo Stock Notes, The Writer,* and *Writer's Digest.*

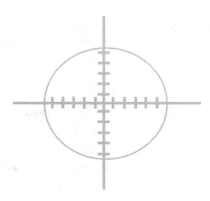

INDEX

BOOKS FROM ALLWORTH PRESS

Writing.com: Creative Internet Strategies to Advance Your Writing Career by Moira Anderson Allen (softcover, 6 × 9, 256 pages, $16.95)

The Complete Guide to Book Marketing by David Cole (softcover, 6 × 9, 288 pages, $19.95)

The Writer's Legal Guide, Second Edition by Tad Crawford and Tony Lyons (hardcover, 6 × 9, 320 pages, $19.95)

The Complete Guide to Book Publicity by Jodee Blanco (softcover, 6 × 9, 288 pages, $19.95)

Writing for Interactive Media: The Complete Guide by Jon Samsel and Darryl Wimberley (hardcover, 6 × 9, 320 pages, $19.95)

The Writer's Internet Handbook, Revised Edition by Timothy K. Maloy (softcover, 6 × 9, 192 pages, $18.95)

How to Write Books That Sell, Second Edition by L. Perry Wilbur and Jon Samsel (hardcover, 6 × 9, 224 pages, $19.95)

How to Write Articles That Sell, Second Edition by L. Perry Wilbur and Jon Samsel (hardcover, 6 × 9, 224 pages, $19.95)

Business and Legal Forms for Authors and Self-Publishers, Revised Edition by Tad Crawford (softcover, 8½ × 11, 192 pages, $18.95)

The Writer's Guide to Corporate Communications by Mary Moreno (softcover, 6 × 9, 192 pages, $18.95)

Mastering the Business of Writing: A Leading Literary Agent Reveals the Secrets of Success by Richard Curtis (softcover, 6 × 9, 272 pages, $18.95)

The Writer's Resource Handbook by Daniel Grant (softcover, 6 × 9, 272 pages, $19.95)